The Dragon Ball Z Legend

How to Use
In this book, the second in the popular **Mysteries and Secrets Revealed!** anime series, you'll find everything you need to know about Dragon Ball Z and much more! And it's so easy to use! Just follow the simple DBZ code below and within a few hours you'll be a Dragon Ball disciple.

Questions and Answers
Want to find out why who did what when and where? Then this is the book for you. 54 questions and detailed answers on every DBZ topic, from characters and relationships to fighting techniques and fusion.

Glossary
When you speak the lingo everything is so much easier. At the back of this book you'll find a glossary stuffed full of names, what they mean and which pages to find them on.

Keyword Index
Want to go straight to Karin's Tower? Then start at the alphabetical Keyword Index at the back of the book. There you'll find page links to every destination in the Dragon Ball world.

DBZ Files
Scattered throughout the book are 10 DBZ Files that introduce you to the wackier side of Dragon Ball mania. Check out the Goku alarm clock, DBZ cosplay, Cell on the cell, DBZ fan interview, who's who, the $30-billion industry, and DBZ wallets, pouches, guitar picks and figures!

CONTENTS

Training, Time Travel and Killer Techniques

Family, Friends and Nauseous Foes

Back in the Real World...

✪✪✪✪✪ DBZ Files ✪✪✪✪✪

From Kung Fu to Yoikominminken

Dragon Ball is the brainchild of Akira Toriyama, a big fan of Kung Fu movies, especially *Enter the Dragon* and *Drunken Master*, and in the hugely popular story, dramatic fight scenes are what keeps the action flowing.

The Dragon Ball manga series began its serialization in the weekly comic *Shonen Jump*, published by Shueisha, in the autumn of 1984. It's no secret that the character of Son Goku, Dragon Ball's hero, is taken from *Saiyuki*, the classical Chinese saga in which the main character is a mischievous monkey named Songoku. This provided Akira Toriyama with a basic model from which to work. At first, he created a Goku that was very similar to the original Songoku. But the similarities, he decided, were too obvious, and in the end only Goku's tail remained as a clue to his origins.

By that stage, Toriyama was already a well-known and popular comic artist, thanks to the success of Doctor Slump. However, Dragon Ball was not an immediate success, ranking low in reader polls. It was only with the introduction of the Tenkaichi Tournaments that its popularity soared.

The tale begins when Goku and

Saiyuki (1960,Toei) Poster $80.00

Buruma first meet. Goku is persuaded to help Buruma in her quest to find the seven dragon balls. With these, she hopes to call up the magic dragon, Shenlong, and be granted one wish - to find her prince charming.

The two set off on their fateful journey, and on the way meet Kamesennin, who gives Goku the Kinto-cloud. They also run into the bad guys Yamcha and Pilaf. Eventually, they manage to collect all seven dragon balls, but lose them to Pilaf, whose wish is for world domination. Oolong, the pig-like character, has other ideas, and makes a wish to Shenlong before Pilaf can get a word in. And what he wishes for is nothing but "A pair of panties worn by some cute girl..."

His wish is Shenlong's command, and Oolong gets exactly what he asks for. In an instant, a single pair of panties drifts down from the sky. This is the very first wish that Shenlong grants in Dragon Ball.

As the story progresses, Goku's opponents get meaner and tougher and the fight scenes become increasingly dramatic. However, the story rarely strays from it comic-book humor.

Once the dragon balls have granted a wish, they turn to stone, are scattered by the four winds, and do not regain their magical powers for an entire year. So Goku decides to take up training under Kamesennin, hoping it will help him track down the dragon balls once again. His fellow student is Kuririn, who will soon become Goku's closest friend.

The world is still at peace, but this shift in the story is probably what sets the tone for later events, where the lead characters undergo rigorous training in order to defeat ever-stronger enemies. Kuririn and Goku use their newly acquired talents to participate in the Tenkaichi Tournament, where they meet the first of their real enemies - The Red Ribbon Army.

It's a tough challenge, but Goku eventually destroys the army and emerges victorious. Tenshinhan and Chaozu enter the 22nd Tournament, the second tournament Goku appears in. It's following this that Piccolo Daimao appears, and sets out to conquer the world. His followers kill Kuririn, who is later resurrected by the dragon balls. Goku also suffers an ignominious defeat at the hands of Daimao. This forces him to climb Karin's Tower and upgrade his power level by drinking the sacred water. He finally acquires enough power to beat Piccolo Daimao.

Majunior (Piccolo), who hatches from an egg that Piccolo Daimao lays from his mouth, participates in the 23rd Tenkaichi Tournament. There, Piccolo faces off against Goku, only to lose. When the tournament is over, the Saiyan Raditz appears. Unknown to Goku, Raditz is actually his elder brother. Raditz kidnaps Gohan, Goku's son, which leads Piccolo to come forward with the offer to help Goku.

Goku eventually defeats Raditz, but before he dies, Raditz predicts that one year from that day his cohorts will attack Earth. Goku sets off to train with Kaiosama in preparation, and is able to defeat Vegeta and his crew when they finally arrive.

However, Goku loses many of his friends, reason enough for Gohan, Kuririn, and Buruma to embark for Planet Namek in the hope of finding the dragon balls. It is there that they meet Freeza, who hopes to gain eternal life with the dragon balls. Vegeta also puts in an appearance, and the scramble for the dragon balls begins. Freeza's private army, the Ginyu Force, turns up and the search becomes a fight to the death.

Goku has trained hard on the long flight to Namek, and defeats the Ginyu Force, leading to a confrontation with Freeza himself. By this time, Goku has become a Super Saiyan, and by sheer strength, he overpowers Freeza. But the defeated Freeza turns into a cyborg and returns a year later for revenge. However, he is given a thrashing by Vegeta and Buruma's son, Trunks, who has come from the future in a time machine.

According to Trunks, the future is a miserable place thanks to the antics of the androids created by Dr. Gero. But a spanner gets thrown into the wheel of time, and it turns out that Androids 16, 17 and 18 are not bad guys at all. They end up battling Cell, the strongest and most evil character to appear so far, to protect the planet and its environment. But Cell is too strong, and moves closer to becoming the perfect being by absorbing every human he comes across. No one is able to stop him, and he even kills Goku. The earth looks set to be destroyed, but Gohan releases a huge Kamehameha that finally kills Cell.

Peace prevails after the death of Goku, but far away on the edge of space Majin Buu, created by the evil wizard Bibidi, is brought back to life. Not only that, but the foolishness of humans works to make Majin Buu even more evil than he originally is. It is Goku, resurrected thanks to Daikaioshin, that defeats Majin Buu with a Genkidama powered by the *ki* energy of all the world's living things. Again, the earth is saved in the eleventh hour.

At the next Tenkaichi Tournament, Goku meets Uub, the reincarnation of Majin Buu, and leads him off on a journey to his southern home where they intend to train together.

From Comic Book to Small-Screen Stardom

The Dragon Ball manga series ended in March 1995. However, the anime broadcast, first aired in February 1986, continued, with Dragon Ball GT, an original anime series, being released in February 1996.

Dragon Ball GT sees the return, after a long absence, of Pilaf and his crew, who bring Piccolo Daimao back to life. Piccolo and his gang collect the Dark Dragon Balls and use them to turn Goku into a child. Goku, Trunks and Pan leave on a journey to retrieve the Dark Dragon Balls and reverse the spell. There they come across numerous enemies, and also run into Evil Shenlong, whose existence is the result of the dragon balls having been overly used. Goku harnesses all the energy of space into the Genkidama to fight off yet another evil dragon, Ii-Shenlong. Goku finally collects all the dragon balls and makes one wish to Shenlong: "To bring everyone back to life." He and Shenlong then disappear. And so the tale, which began with the gathering of the seven dragon balls, ended in November 1997, with the disappearance of those very same dragon balls.

Dragon Ball Takes Over the World

Dragon Ball's popularity skyrocketed while it was still being serialized as a comic. However, the comic books continue to sell in Japan today, with 2002 marking the sale of the 126-millionth copy - one for every person in Japan. Dragon Ball comics have also been released in Hong Kong, Malaysia, Singapore, Thailand, USA, Canada, Brazil, Germany, UK and Belgium, and it's believed that the total number of books in print worldwide has already topped 260 million. If the numerous pirated editions are included, it becomes impossible to count the number of people who have read about Goku and his adventures.

Dragon Ball has become hugely popular in Europe since the anime series was first shown there in 1989. This popularity has led to a number of curious events, such as in Spain, where memorial services are held and a minute of silence observed before the start of soccer matches each time a Dragon Ball character dies on TV.

Dragon Ball was first broadcast on North American TV in 1995 and was picked up by Cartoon Network in 1998. On September 22, 2002, the show recorded the highest viewer rating for the week according to a nationwide TV ratings survey.

Even in Japan, there has been no weakening of DBZ mania, despite the fact that it's almost nine years since the series ended. Spin-offs, such as game software, card games and figures flood the market and the anime series has seen many repeats on TV.

The secret to Dragon Ball's universal success lies in the fact that it's not simply a story of good guys beating bad guys. Although fantasy, Dragon Ball is filled with real-life drama, including how friendships are made and develop, and how bad characters become good and good guys go bad. And all of this is played out with a cheerful tongue-in-cheek optimism.

The scale of the story also sets it apart from would-be imitators. Let's not forget that in Dragon Ball there are some characters that outrank God in terms of both power and influence. In fact, there are moments when the story seems to have outgrown itself and gotten completely out of hand. But this is where the author, Akira Toriyama, shows his true genius, neatly tying up the narrative's loose ends and bringing it all back under control...until the next battle begins.

Little Screen, Big Screen - The Dragon Ball
Anime Legend

Television

Dragon Ball   Broadcast in Japan - February 1986 to April 1989

An exciting story of the search for the seven dragon balls, magic stones capable of granting any wish. Includes the meeting of Goku and Buruma, how Goku trains with Kuririn under Kamesennin, and the many adventures that they and other characters, such as Yamcha and Oolong, have. Introduces ever-stronger opponents, such as the Red Ribbon Army, Tao Pai-Pai, Tenshinhan and Piccolo Daimao, who engage in high-powered battles with Goku.

Dragon Ball Z   Broadcast in Japan - April 1989 to January 1996

Five years on from the fierce battles of the Tenkaichi Tournaments, the world has achieved peace. Goku and his wife Chi-Chi have been blessed with a son, Gohan, and live each day in happiness. But peace comes to a sudden end with the arrival of Goku's elder brother, Raditz, and his powerful tail. Raditz intends to annihilate all humans on the face of the planet, and to make this possible kidnaps Gohan and takes him hostage, demanding that Goku join his Saiyan brothers in their quest for destruction. Goku joins forces with his erstwhile rival Piccolo Daimao to fight Raditz. But it is the power of Gohan that bursts forth, coming to his father's rescue and setting the scene for the exploits of Son Gohan.

Dragon Ball GT   Broadcast in Japan - February 1996 to November 1997

Goku and Uub face off in a graduation fight in the Cosmos. But while the fierce battle ensues, Pilaf and his gang, previous rivals of Goku in his search for the dragon balls, slip into the temple where the dragon balls are kept. They attempt to smuggle out the set in order to realize their dream of ruling the world. Goku gets wind of what's happening but is turned into a child by Pilaf using the power of the dragon balls. The balls disperse into space once their magic has been used. However, these dragon balls are special. If not recovered within a year, the earth will disappear!

Television Specials

Dragon Ball Z Bardock Story: Lonely Final Battle...
Broadcast in Japan - October 17, 1990

A story centering on Bardock, Goku's father. Bardock rebels against Freeza, who has betrayed him and wants to destroy Planet Vegeta and his fellow Saiyans. Bardock is killed in the end, but not before he sees the future, where Goku destroys Freeza.

13

Dragon Ball Z Trunks Story

Broadcast in Japan - February 24, 1993

In the future reign of terror led by the androids, Gohan and Trunks' opposition is futile. In time, Gohan himself is killed, and so Trunks sets off on a journey that will change history.

Dragon Ball GT Special:
Goku's Supplement! Proof of Courage is the Four-Star Dragon Ball

Broadcast in Japan - March 26 1997

100 hundred years has passed since Son Goku vanquished his opponent, the mutant Baby. The earth has recovered some semblance of peace, but Goku and his friends are nowhere to be seen. Indeed, the only one left is the 100-year-old Pan, daughter of Gohan and Videl, who lives with her great-great-great-grandchild Goku Jr. To all appearances, Goku Jr. looks just like Goku, but in fact he's a weakling, bullied by those around him. This is the story of his search for the dragon balls.

Movies

Dragon Ball: Shenron no Densetsu (1986, Toei)
Dragon Ball: Curse of the Blood Rubies `50 min`

The memorable first movie-theater release introducing many new characters. In a faraway land, the King Gurumes is terrorizing the countryside to mine blood rubies. The king is cursed, and needs the rubies so that he can buy the only cure - the seven mystic dragon balls. A little girl named Penny sets out to find the great Master Roshi to save her village, which is being destroyed by the ruby mining. On her way, she comes across a huge ogre but is saved by Goku. Goku and Buruma are also looking for the dragon balls, but decide to help Penny in her mission. Goku must take on King Gurumes and his evil underlings Pasta and Bongo.

Dragon Ball: Mashinjo no Nemuri Hime (1987, Toei)
Dragon Ball: Sleeping Princess in Devil's Castle `45 min`

Goku sets out for the Devil's Castle with Kuririn on the orders of Kamesennin to rescue the sleeping beauty trapped there. They enter the castle and there starts a series of wild fights with different monsters and devils. Buruma, who has followed Goku, gets caught by the demon king Lucifer. The sleeping beauty turns out to be a jewel, with which Lucifer is attempting to destroy the sun, using the power of the jewel and a lightning cannon. However, Goku suddenly changes into a giant monkey and saves Kuririn and the rest. Lucifer lets fly with the lightning cannon but Goku lets rip with the Kamehameha.

Dragon Ball: Makafushigi Daiboken (1988, Toei)
Dragon Ball: Mystical Adventure 46 min

Goku is meant to participate in the martial arts tournament in the Mifan Empire. But the bride of Emperor Chaozu, Ran Ran, has gone missing. Chaozu's faithful minister attempts to rally the troops in order to find the dragon balls so the emperor's wish may be granted. However, the truth is that Tao Pai-Pai has teamed up with Tenshinhan to conquer the world. Bora, who possesses the last dragon ball, pleads with the emperor to stop the fighting, but is chased away. Goku promises to talk to the emperor in his place, if Bora wins the tournament. But just as Bora looks set to win the tournament, Tao Pai-Pai appears and makes a nuisance of himself. Goku attacks but is done in by the Dodonpa. Goku goes on the offensive after being saved by Karin and winning the help of Arare-chan and Gacchanz at Penguin Village.

Dragon Ball Z (1989, Toei)
Dragon Ball Z 40 min

The movie tells the story of the battle between Goku and his long-standing enemy, Garlic Jr. A mysterious threesome suddenly arrives in the mountains where Gohan is growing up healthy and strong, and steal away not only with Gohan, but also with three dragon balls. Goku hears about this, borrows the Dragon Radar from Buruma, and sets out to find Gohan. By this stage, Garlic Jr. has managed to gather together all seven dragon balls and has achieved eternal life. Goku arrives on the scene and a fierce battle ensues with the mysterious three. Goku wins out with the help of Kuririn and Piccolo, to face off with Garlic, who has grown to gigantic proportions. Gohan bursts into tears at the sight, but the light that emerges from him works to encase Garlic in a black hole.

Dragon Ball Z: Konoyo de Ichiban Tsuyoi Yatsu (1990 Toei)
Dragon Ball Z: The World's Strongest 60 min

The location is the Tsurumaitsuruburi mountains, which are capped in eternal snow and glaciers. Oolong and Gohan have picked up the search for the dragon balls on the Dragon Radar, and hurry to the mountain peak, but Shenlong has already upped and gone. It is none other than the evil scientist Dr. Kochin who has managed to gather the balls together and send Shenlong away. In order to conquer the world, Kochin has also managed to bring back to life Dr. Wheelo, who has survived for 50 years as just a brain preserved deep in the ice. Dr. Wheelo arrives at the Kame House some weeks later, and takes Kamesennin and Buruma off to the Tsurumaitsuruburi mountains. When Goku hears of this, he rushes to the mountain peak to save them. But there waiting for him is Piccolo, who is being controlled by dark forces...

Dragon Ball Z: Chikyu Marugoto Cho Kessen (1990 Toei)
Dragon Ball Z: The Ultimate Decisive Battle for Earth 60 min

A sinister space-force led by the vicious and cruel Taurus encroaches on peaceful Earth. Taurus aims to take over all of space, and has assumed vast powers by eating the fruit of the Tree of Power, the Shinseiju. Taurus attempts to grow the tree on Earth. The truth is that once the tree takes root, it draws all power from the soil in which it is planted, and grows until it leaves the planet a desolate desert. Goku and the Z Warriors know of this, and attempt to put a stop to Taurus' plans. But Taurus reacts by sending his minions out to rid him of the meddlesome Z Warriors.

Dragon Ball Z: Super Saiyan da Songoku (1991 Toei)
Dragon Ball Z: The Super Saiyan is Songoku `50 min.`

Goku sees a strange planet approaching the earth. He flies
way up into the air with Kuririn in an attempt to alter the
planet's orbit, but is thrust back to Earth and suffers a near-
fatal injury. Lord Slug of the Nameks attacks Earth from the
planet. Gohan fights bravely to save the earth without
knowing the whereabouts of Goku, but he loses his precious
dragon ball. Slug, who realizes the power of the dragon
balls, hunts down the remaining balls and calls forth
Shenlong, recovering his eternal youth and power as a
result. With his powers regained, Slug engulfs the earth in a
black gas, transforming it into a world of ice.

**Dragon Ball Z: The Super Saiyan is Songoku
Program $5.00**

Dragon Ball Z: Tobikiri no Saikyo Vs. Saikyo (1991 Toei)
Dragon Ball Z: Battle of the Strongest vs. the Strongest `47 min.`

Goku, Gohan, Kuririn, Oolong, Buruma, and Haiya Dragon are enjoying a camping trip when they
are attacked by Cooler, the elder brother of Freeza, the killer of Goku's father 20 years earlier. In
turn, it was Goku who defeated Freeza, and now Cooler has arrived to avenge his brother. Goku
puts up a fierce defense against a surprise attack by Sauza, Doole and Neiz, Cooler's hired guns.
But he's overwhelmed by Cooler's huge power and tumbles into a bottomless ravine. Cooler
seizes on this chance to destroy Earth. Goku has been knocked out, but is found by Gohan and
Kuririn. Gohan then sets out for Karin's Tower on the back of Haiya Dragon in an attempt to
obtain the Senzu Beans and save Goku.

Dragon Ball Z: Gekitotsu!! 100 Oku Pawa no Senshitachi (1992 Toei)
Dragon Ball Z: Attack!! The Ten-Billion-Power Warriors `45 min.`

Goku and friends have gone off to save
Namek, which has been attacked by a
mechanical planet. What they find upon
their arrival is Metal Cooler, who, after
being defeated by Goku, was brought
back to life as a cyborg. Again, they
come to blows. But Goku is badly hurt
and looks set to meet his maker when his
longtime rival Vegeta plucks him from the
jaws of death. Goku somehow manages
to overcome Metal Cooler, and he and his
friends destroy the mechanical planet
with the help of Vegeta.

**Dragon Ball Z: The Ten-Billion-Power Warriors
Program $5.00**

Dragon Ball Z: Kyokugen Batoru!! Sandai Super Saiyan (1993 Toei)
Dragon Ball Z: Battle Limit!! Three Great Super Saiyans `45 min.`

Dr. Gero, who tries to destroy Goku, is killed by the androids he created. However, the data he leaves behind produces the most powerful androids, numbers 13, 14 and 15. Androids 14 and 15 launch a surprise attack against Goku and his friends, who are relaxing in Ginza, which sends bystanders into a panic. Goku and Trunks fear for the innocent people around them, so shift the fight to the glacier region, while leaving Kuririn and Gohan to take care of everyone else. However, their movements have been tracked by the computer, and they're soon on the defensive and unable to recover lost ground. But Vegeta appears just in the nick of time. The three great Super Saiyans - Goku, Trunks and Vegeta - are now assembled in full force, and resume their fight to the death.

Dragon Ball Z: Moetsukiro!! Nessen Ressen Cho-gekisen (1993 Toei)
Dragon Ball Z: Burning spirits! Violent Fight! Super Exciting Fight `70 min.`

Planet Vegeta, long ago destroyed by Freeza, is reborn as a new star. Paragas, who once served King Vegeta, now looks to welcome Prince Vegeta back as king in order to have him defeat the Super Saiyans, who threaten the new planet. Vegeta suspects nothing as he heads to the new planet. Meanwhile, Goku uses his *ki* to search space in an attempt to defeat the Super Saiyans who are rampaging at the behest of Kaio. Goku somehow manages to make it to the new planet and meets again with Vegeta, Gohan and Kuririn. In actual fact, it is the son of Paragas, Broly, who is the legendary Super Saiyan, and Paragas plots to use Broly to gain control over the earth.

Dragon Ball Z: Burning spirits! Violent Fight! Super Exciting Fight
Program $3.00

Dragon Ball Z: Ginga Giri!! Buchigirino Sugoi-yatsu (1993 Toei)
Dragon Ball Z: The Galaxy Is in Danger!! The Super-Awesome Guy `50 min.`

The legends of the martial arts world come from every corner of the planet to take part in the Tenkaichi Tournament. These include Gohan, Trunks, Kuririn and Piccolo. But Mister Satan's pupils, who were supposed to fight in the semi-finals, are all killed. And in their place await Gokua, Bido, Bujin and Zangya, the henchmen of Bojack, the vicious warrior looking to conquer the earth. Tenshinhan, Yamcha and Vegeta all fall before their power, but Gohan is transformed into a Super Saiyan with the encouragement of his father, Goku, who is in Heaven. Gohan routs his opponents.

Dragon Ball Z: Kiken na Futari! Super Senshi wa Nemurenai (1994 Toei)
Dragon Ball Z: Mischievous Partners! Super-Warriors Never Rest `50 min.`

Goten, Trunks and Videl set out on a search for the dragon balls and arrive at the village of Natade. The villagers are concerned both by the sudden change in climate and the appearance of a monster, to which they're considering sacrificing a young girl named Coco. But Goten and his friends do away with the monster with little effort, and save the village. Who should appear then but the reincarnation of Broly, the legendary Super Saiyan that Goku defeated seven years before. There is little that Goten and his friends can do but defend themselves. Their backs are soon against the wall in the face of Broly's overpowering strength, but at that very moment the seven dragon balls resonate in unison and Goten's father, Goku, who is dead, comes back to life.

Dragon Ball Z: Cho-senshi Gekiha!! Katsunowa Oreda (1994 Toei)
Dragon Ball Z: Destruct Super Warriors!! Winner is Me `45 min.`

Jagga Batta Danshaku, the childhood friend of Mr. Satan, sends him a challenge after the latter wins the Tenkaichi Tournament. Android 18, who is looking to pick up his promised bribe from Mr. Satan, arrives at Jagga's mansion at the same time as Goten, Trunks and Satan. A number of scientists are working to produce a bio-warrior, and Broly, the guy Goten fought so hard to beat, is going to be one of them. It looks as though not even Android 18, Goten, Trunks and Kuririn can make any impression on Broly, who has been revitalized as the strongest bio-warrior. But a last-minute blast of inspiration from Trunks sees them lure him towards a tank full of chemicals that can dissolve anything.

Dragon Ball Z: Fukkatsu no Fusion!! Goku to Vegeta (1995 Toei)
Dragon Ball Z: The Resurrection of Fusion!! Goku and Vegeta `45 min.`

Aka-oni, who works in the palace of Enma, goofs off. This leads to the Spirit Laundry exploding, which exposes Aka-oni to an evil spirit that transforms him into Janemba. Not even Enma Daio can prevail against the awesome powers of Janemba, and Goku and Pikko, who are training hard in the Nether World, are called upon to help. But they are also unable to defeat Janemba, even when they combine their powers. To make things worse, a spate of incidents occurs where the dead return to life. Goten and Trunks investigate, but it's all too much for them. They ask for Shenlong's help, but he refuses, saying his powers do not extend to the Nether World.

Dragon Ball Z: Ryuken Bakuhatsu! Goku ga Yaraneba Dare Ga Yaru (1995 Toei)
Dragon Ball Z: Dragon Fist Assault!! If Goku Can't Do It, Who Can? `52 min.`

Gohan and Videl meet the mysterious old-timer Hoi, who tells them of a strange music box. The story is that a legendary warrior resides in the box. Gohan wants to have a look, but no one seems to be able to open the music box. So they decide to use Shenlong's strength. First they collect all the dragon balls before calling him and getting him to open the music box. The awakened warrior Tapion, however, is angered that he has been aroused from his slumbers. And worse is to come. That same night a monster made up of nothing but legs goes on a rampage, then suddenly disappears. Goku and his friends must find out what lies behind the mystery of the legendary warrior and the monster sealed in his body.

Dragon Ball Z: Saikyo eno Michi (1996 Toei)
Dragon Ball Z: Tenth Anniversary Movie `80 min.`

Buruma, who has managed to collect two of the legendary dragon balls, meets Son Goku, who has one as a gift from his grandfather. They decide to join forces, and set off on a search for the other dragon balls. On their journey, they come under attack from Yamcha and Puar, and also have a run-in with Android 18. But worse it yet to come. The Red Ribbon Army suddenly attack, and all but Goku are captured. Commander Red, who possesses the seventh ball, seizes the other five from Buruma before setting out to lure Goku and the one remaining ball into a trap. Produced as a tenth anniversary celebration, this was the last of the Dragon Ball movies.

Dragon Ball Z: Tenth Anniversary Movie
Program $3.00

Training, Time Travel and Killer Techniques

Dragon Ball Collection Vol.1
Goku
$2.00

Where and when do the Dragon Ball stories take place? 01

The setting for Dragon Ball is evidently Planet Earth - the author admits as much on the cover of the first volume of the comic book. Still, while there is an underlying Chinese feel to the setting, there is nothing in the story that actually indicates it takes place in China.

This also goes for the period. At the very start of the manga, there is a passage that says, "It happened long, long ago. On a mountain thousands of miles far beyond the towns and cities...These are the beginnings of this surreal tale."

But having said that, characters such as Buruma have control over technologies that are simply not possible under existing scientific limitations. This suggests that the setting is far in the future. However, dinosaurs pop up out of nowhere, only adding to the difficulty of pinning the story to any one particular era.

Earth is comprised of a single nation ruled by a king, who, oddly enough, is a dog.

See Glossary

King

He has the intellectual abilities of a human being and, as such, speaks like one. But there is no mistaking the canine features of his face. He lives in a fortress called, fittingly enough, King's Castle, where he is protected by guards. He is the leader of a military force known as the Royal Defense Forces.

To the unknowing eye, Earth appears to be at peace. But there are many villains at large, such as the Rabbit Army and Red Dragon. What's more, these guys are able to muster a military strength to rival the royal forces. This is one crazy, topsy-turvy world!

Interestingly, the currency is known *zeni*, the way money is sometimes referred to in Japan. (while the currency of Japan is yen, small change is still referred to a "kozeni.")

See Glossary
Royal Defense Forces
Rabbit Army
Zeni

See questions

7 12 13 20

What is a dragon ball?

02

A dragon ball is a softly glowing orb that can sit neatly in the palm of the hand but contains fragments of stars. There are seven such balls in total, and the story goes that if all seven dragon balls are collected and magic words uttered then the Dragon God will appear to grant the holder a wish...any wish at all.

One thing that must be remembered is that once the wish is granted, the dragon balls turn into worthless stones that are scattered far and wide. They do not recover their power and shape as dragon balls for a full year. That pretty much sums up the story of the dragon balls created by Kamisama in the first half of the tale. However, three different kinds of dragon balls appear as the story progresses.

Firstly, there are Kamisama's Dragon Balls. As has just been explained, these balls grant a single wish. If that wish is to bring back to life those whose deaths were the result of murder or battle, and not natural causes such as sickness or old age, then it's possible to bring any number of people back to life at the same time.

However, the wish will be not be granted for people who have been dead longer than a year. Nor is it possible to make the same wish twice, meaning the same person cannot be brought back to life time and time again.

The second kind of dragon balls are the original balls from the Planet Namek. The Namek Dragon Balls grant three wishes, but it's only possible to bring one person back to life. Still, unlike the dragon balls from Earth, the Namek Dragon Balls allow the bearer to bring the same person back time after time, as long as they didn't succumb to death by natural causes.

The third and final type of dragon balls are the Dende Dragon Balls, which grant two wishes. It's possible to bring many people back to life at the same time with the Dende Dragon Balls, but if they die again then they can no longer be revived.

We can therefore see that the powers of each set of dragon balls are somewhat different, and that there is a contradiction in saying the dragon balls will grant all and every kind of wish. In a tale of such scope and magnitude, it comes as little surprise to find more than a few contradictions.

See Glossary

Planet Namek

See questions

14 19 20 24
26 28 29 32
36 39 40 46
47 48

There are many power attacks, but which is the most powerful? **03**

Each warrior has his attack technique of choice. For Goku, it's the Kamehameha and the Genkidama. For Kuririn, it's the Kienzan; for Kamesennin, the Niju Zanzoken; and for Tenshinhan, the Shinkikoho. Android 16 uses the Hell's Flash; Vegeta the Galic Gun, Big Bang Attack and the Final Flash; and Piccolo uses the Makkankosappo, or Special Beam Cannon.

Goku and Kuririn employ *ki* energy in their power attacks, in common with many moves in the series. Attacks, such as the Kamehameha, which "concentrate latent energy residing in the body, releasing it in a single burst," use the *ki* energy that is within us all.

Freeza's specialty is attacks or moves that use supernatural power. The difference between this and *ki* is that while we're all capable of using the latter in some shape or form, only a very small number of people are gifted with supernatural power.

Then there are the energy waves used by

See Glossary

Genkidama
Kienzan
Shinkikoho
Android
Hell's Flash
Galic Gun
Final Flash
Makkankosappo

25

the androids. Androids use energy created in internally installed reactors to create special weapons.

So, which is the most powerful? Well, the attacks have never all been employed at the same time and in the same place, so it's difficult to make precise comparisons.

But remember what happens to the Kamehameha: In the latter part of the series, it's souped up to such an extent that it blows Earth away!

This is consistent with the storyline, which has Goku steadily increasing his fighting powers so as to be able to take on newer and more powerful opponents as they appear.

In this respect, the most powerful DBZ force may well be the Genkidama that floors the last great enemy - Majin Buu. That's also true in the sense that while it's Goku who releases the Genkidama, the weapon itself is a concentration of the *ki* of billions of people and natural elements spread across the earth, something that cannot be repeated too often. With this in mind, it's probably correct to call Genkidama the ultimate power attack.

See questions

16 17 22 24
25 27 31 32
34 38

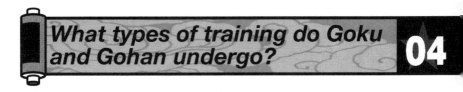

What types of training do Goku and Gohan undergo?

04

G oku's first experience of real training is under the supervision of Kamesennin. This is simply because Goku wants to become stronger, and not to fight any specific enemy. The training takes place in a number of locations that at the same time introduces many different terrains, such as a tropical island, the desert and the jungle.

Kuririn undergoes the same training. He is sent out to isolated locations, such as glaciers and deserts that are usually only accessible by helicopter, and told to get to his destination "before the milk turns sour." This training also sees Kuririn strengthen his back by working in the fields, and doing exercises that harden even the tips of his fingers. He earns money through building work and hones his reflexes by deflecting an attack by killer bees on top of everything else.

While all this is going on, Goku is shouldering a 40 kg turtle shell. As a result, he is able to move huge boulders and leap higher than the clouds.

There's also the training conducted by Karin, which takes place at his tower some-where above the clouds that nobody has entered since Master Roshi some 300 years before. Just getting there adds enormous strength to the legs and lower back.

This training consists of attempting to chase down what Karin calls his sacred water, which flits off this way and that. All this swift, quick-turning, jerky movement is very much like a game of tag, and helps the student to become extremely agile. Of course, nobody realizes that the sacred water is just plain H20...but that probably adds to the excitement.

The real sacred water has the power to make people sleepy, but it eventually kills most who drink it. Goku, however, drinks the water to build up his immunity and increase his powers.

The training conducted by Kami takes place in God's Palace hovering even higher in the sky than Karin's Tower. Those chosen by Karin are allowed to ascend to the palace using the Nyoi Bo, or Power Pole, an extending cane.

This workout begins with disciplining the spirit by undergoing Zen meditation and clearing one's mind of all concerns. This translates into increased speeds by eradicating all unnec-

See Glossary

Sacred water
Karin's Tower
Nyoi Bo

essary movement, allowing the trainee to release his power in concentrated bursts by mastering the technique of maximizing effect and minimizing movement.

As a result, the trainee is endowed with a radically different set of fighting techniques than what he could learn on Earth, allowing him to sense the presence of his adversaries intuitively and blast them with shock waves. It's after completing this training that Goku wins his first championship at the Tenkaichi Tournament.

The training conducted by Kaiosama takes place on Kaio Planet, a very small planet that has ten times the gravitational pull of Earth.

The training begins with attempts to catch Bubbles, Kaio's extremely agile pet monkey. Chasing him helps develop the kind of physical power that can overcome gravity, and, by mastering the delicate control of the spirit and concentrating the animus - the get-up-and-go - of all living things, allows the trainee to let rip with the Genkidama.

Goku masters Kaioken - a technique devised by Kaio. And the newly powered-up Goku manages to return along the Snake Way, which took him six months to first travel along, in just a day and a half!

The training of young Gohan conducted

See Glossary

Tenkaichi Tournament
Bubbles
Genkidama
Kaioken

by Piccolo takes place on a rock-strewn wasteland. It is an extreme, Spartan training that consists of such painful activities as throwing oneself at rocks. But it leads to the development of both his body and spirit. This allows Gohan to later survive in such severe environments as those inhabited by dinosaurs.

Gohan's training ranges from the physical to the mental, requiring exercises of the body before moving on to one-to-one training that allows for control of the mind. Gohan does nothing but cry at first, but after a year of this rigorous workout, he becomes a full-fledged warrior, with fighting capabilities and techniques to match.

See questions

7 16 17 22 24 26

Dragon Ball Collection Vol.1
Gohan (Super Saiyan)
$2.00

What is a Scouter?

The Saiyan Raditz is the first to use the Scouter. Clipped over one ear, the Scouter is a compact device that gives a numerical value to the fighting capabilities of an opponent when seen through its single lens.

When Raditz comes to Earth and finds that the fighting power of the average human male is a mere 5, he considers mankind to be almost worthless. When a few humans then try to kill him with a shot from a rifle, Raditz catches the bullet and, flicking it back with his fingertips, kills the shooter.

At this stage in the story, the fighting capability of Goku is measured at 334, at 419 when he removes his heavy clothes, and 924 when he lets rip with the Kamehameha. However, Goku's fighting power increases as he undergoes all sorts of training that will help him against his enemies.

According to one series editor, "...the creator, Akira Toriyama, picked up many ideas from different sources. The Scouter itself is a good example, as it comes from a video game."

See Glossary
Scouter

See questions

16 17 18

DBZ File

001

Wakey Wakey!

If you're having trouble getting out of bed in the morning, then this ingenious alarm clock in the shape of Goku surfing through the skies on his Kinto-cloud is just the thing for you.

When it's time to peel open those crusty eyelids and face another day, the 6-inch-high digital clock starts up an infernal rendition of the Dragon Ball theme tune that'll soon have your neighbors wishing they lived in Belgium. And if that's not enough, and for many of us it isn't, a motor within the cloud sends cute little Goku careering in circles across the room in a manner that is downright psychotic at that hour in the morning.

Fortunately, a switch on top turns the damn thing off. However, if there's an open window close by, don't hesitate to chuck little Goku into the street and return to your own cloud in the sky.

Morning Musuko: Son Goku Alarm Clock
$22.00
http://www.banpresto.co.jp/
© Bird Studio/Shueisha - Toei Animation

How long is the Snake Way that leads to Kaio's Planet? 06

The Snake Way is the route Raditz, Goku's elder brother, uses in his assault on Earth when he attempts to destroy all living creatures.

Goku joins with Piccolo to fight Raditz, but they're not strong enough, forcing Piccolo to kill both Raditz and Goku with his Makankosappo.

His intention is to bring Goku back to life using the dragon balls, but while he's dead, Goku is taken by Kamisama to the palace of Enma Daio. Kamisama requests Goku be allowed to undertake training with Kaio, and they set off for Kaio's Planet after their wish is granted.

According to the guide at the gate to the Snake Way, legend has it that the road is about one million kilometers long, and that over the last 100 million years the only person to have reached Kaio's retreat is Enma Daio.

Dark clouds hang over the road, so it's difficult to see what lies ahead, and Hell lies

See Glossary

Makankosappo

below, so there's no coming back if you fall!

Goku has not considered this proposal too seriously, and, using Bukujutsu, takes a flying leap into the air. He soon regrets this, as he puts so much power into the jump that he risks losing the energy needed to complete the journey.

Goku falls into a state of exhaustion and it takes him six months to complete the journey to Kaio's small planet. However, Goku eventually acquires awesome powers as a result of his training with Kaio, including mastering the Kaioken.

When he leaves, Goku skips back down the road it took him six months to previously travel along in just over a day exclaiming, "Wow! I feel so light. My body is as light as cotton wool!"

See Glossary
Kaioken

See questions
2 4 17 18
27

What are the Tenkaichi Tournaments? **07**

Master Roshi says in passing to his two pupils, Goku and Kuririn, "You both show promise. You know, if you continue to train hard, there's a chance you could take part in the tournament eight months from now." He is referring to the Tenkaichi Tournament.

Kuririn's eyes light up, and he exclaims, "Wow! That's the tournament that brings together nothing but the best in martial arts experts from all over the kingdom to decide just who is the greatest in the land!"

The Tenkaichi Tournaments take place once every several years in the south of the Dragon Ball world. The preliminaries take place in the Martial Arts Hall, which is closed to the general public. The participants draw lots, are separated into groups, and face off to decide who will qualify for the tournament proper. The bouts at the hall are held one-on-one, and fighters who fall from the ring, faint, give up or burst into tears are deemed losers. Killing one's oppo-

See Glossary
Tenkaichi Tournament

nent or using weapons results in disqualification.

The general public is admitted to the main tournament, which is once again held in a ring with the bouts decided by lots. The bouts are held one-on-one with no time limits, with the losers being those who fall from the ring, say "Give up!", or, in the case of being knocked down, are unable to get up again during a 10-count. Killing opponents, using weapons, gouging eyes and attacking the vitals are all against the rules.

The tournament that Goku and Kuririn first participate in is the 21st in the series. Goku, while being the youngest participant, makes it all the way to the final. He is beaten by the craftiness of Master Roshi, who participates in the guise of Jackie Chun.

The 22nd Tournament is, effectively, a face-off between the two schools, Kamesenryu and Tsurusenryu. Tsurusennin burns with a desire for revenge against Kamesennin. However, his pupil Tenshinhan wants to prove his worth as a martial artist by fighting fair-and-square with Goku, and goes against his master's decree to engage in foul play. It is a strong fight, but luck is with Tenshinhan, who defeats Goku.

The tables are turned in the 23rd Tournament, when Goku and Chi-Chi meet in the first round of the tournament proper. Goku defeats Chi-Chi, following which they up and get married!

Goku once again makes it to the final where he struggles to overcome the sheer size of Majunior. He succeeds in winning his first tournament after mustering all his strength to release a flying Bukujutsu blow.

The level of the tournaments deteriorates in the period that follows, and Goku and his friends choose not to participate. This changes when Gohan turns 17, and the tournament returns to its former glory.

Goku's second son, Goten, shows incredible strength in the youth tournament, and faces off in the final against Trunks, only to lose. However, these two then join forces, with one climbing onto the other's shoulders to become Mighty Mask, and sneak into the open tournament.

The final is between Android 18 and Mr. Satan, with the vast difference in strength clear to all who watch. However, Android 18 takes the fall, after Mr. Satan agrees to give him 20 million zeni - or twice the amount of the prize money.

In the final episode of the series, Goku comes up against Uub, the reincarnation of Majin Buu.

See Glossary

Mighty Mask
Android
Zeni
Uub

See questions

1	4	8	9
10	12	16	17
21	22	24	31
34	43	44	46

DBZ File

002

DBZ 100-Dollar Make-Over

Tired of dressing up in the same old bed-sheet every Halloween? Don't have anything to wear at the next cosplay event? Wanna get more respect from the kids on the block? Well, worry no more, because Tokyo's Cospa has the ideal solution to your what-to-wear blues. For a mere 100 bucks, you can now look exactly like your hero Goku (sans the hairstyle) with this newly released Kamesenryu fighting suit.

In three sizes that fit almost all, this orange Goku suit emblazoned with the Kame mark is the top-selling item in Cospa's new TRAN TRIP line of anime costumes. The suit is both durable and easy-to-wear, and comes with all the extras, including under-shirt, belt, boots and wristbands. What's more, it's made with the discerning fighter in mind. Because the suit is washable, you'll never have to worry again about being splashed with your opponent's blood.

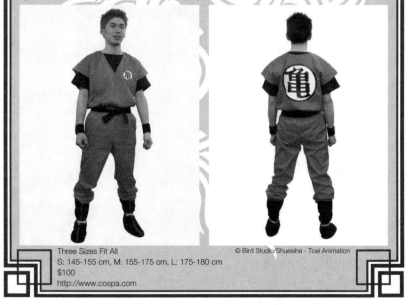

Three Sizes Fit All
S: 145-155 cm, M: 155-175 cm, L: 175-180 cm
$100
http://www.cospa.com

© Bird Studio/Shueisha - Toei Animation

which is so powerful it blows away the ring! But Goku escapes by the skin of his teeth by leaping into the sky. He then uses all his remaining strength to release the Kamehameha, and, propelled by the power of the wave, head-butts Tenshinhan!

Tenshinhan faints and it looks as though Goku is going to win after he follows up with a small Kamehameha. Instead, he collides with a passing car, and as Goku has overstepped the ring he is declared the loser.

Following the bout, Tenshinhan gallantly admits that, "Judged on merit alone, I would have to say I lost the fight," and he offers half the prize money to Goku.

At the 23rd Tournament, there are a series of intriguing match-ups, including Tenshinhan and Tao Pai-Pai, and a repeat match between Tenshinhan and Goku. After the preliminaries, the final is fought between Goku and Majunior.

"Don't worry about saying goodbye to your friends. I will send them all to the land of the dead just as soon as I have killed you," Majunior says. Against this, Goku is just his same old self, saying, "Haven't fought this guy before, so I'm not really that confident."

It turns into a bout of ultra high power techniques, but Goku stops short of releasing the Super Kamehameha, as it would kill not only Majunior but also Kamisama. However, once he realizes he can use the dragon balls to bring back to life everyone killed, including Kuririn, his true fighting mode kicks in.

Majunior expands to massive proportions, which is bad news for Goku. But Goku uses the diversion to rescue Kamisama. As the fight rages, they both suffer serious injuries, but in the end, it is Goku who emerges victorious after he swoops out of the sky to hit Majunior with all his might, bouncing him out of the ring.

For a time, Goku and his friends choose not to participate in the tournaments, although it's probably more accurate to say they have no time to spare as they're off fighting to protect the earth or in training. When they do return after a long absence, Gohan and Trunks engage in a supercharged battle, which Trunks, the elder by a year, wins by a whisker.

See questions
2 7 9 17
22

What are some of the weirder bouts at the Tenkaichi Tournament?

09

While there have been many memorable fights at the Tenkaichi Tournament, there have also been a number of unusual bouts and bloopers. The face-off between Kuririn and Bacterian at the 21st Tournament will be remembered as one that gave us all a good laugh.

Bacterian, of course, is the guy who hasn't washed himself since the day he was born, and looks to use this to overpower his opponents with the disgusting stink from his mouth and groin!

When he has Kuririn on the canvas, he attempts to do him in with an SBD - a Silent But Deadly fart - and a final kick. Goku comes to the rescue, shouting to the reeling Kuririn, "The smell is all in your mind! There's no way he can smell like that! You don't even have a nose!"

On hearing this, Kuririn springs up from the canvas, drops Bacterian with a single kick and farts in his face! That's enough for

See Glossary
Tenkaichi Tournament

Bacterian.

Another classic is the first round match of the tournament that sees Goku and his friends participate after their long absence. In this, the bout between Kuririn and Punter is totally one-sided.

The obese Punter exclaims, "I'm going to show you that the Tenkaichi Tournament isn't just a game! Go ahead, try throwing a punch! What are you waiting for?" Kuririn answers this with a simple, "Okay then," and while looking away boots both sides of Punter's face, blasting him out of the ring.

The final bout of the tournament between Mr. Satan and Android 18 is also one of those bizarre events seldom seen.

Mr. Satan is quaking in his boots from the outset, pleading with Android 18, "Please, don't kill me. I'll do anything you say." Android 18 answers him by saying, "I could let you have the championship. Just give me 20 million zeni, and I'll take the fall for you!"

Mr. Satan agrees to the deal, and punches Android 18 with all his might, screaming, "Satan Miracle Special Ultra Super Megaton Punch!" Android 18 doesn't budge an inch. "Is that it? Is that your killer-punch?" he asks Satan, who replies, "Well, that's about all I've got." Then suddenly Android 18 throws himself

See Glossary
Android
Zeni

out of the ring!

Mr. Satan watches this, then declares, "Well, let's see. Yes, that was one of those punches that don't look like much at first, but gives you the wobbles a few seconds later!" And if that wasn't enough, he shouts, "That was Satan, Miracle, Peachful Boom-Boom!"

Satan takes the applause, but Android 18 whispers in his ear, "I'll be round at your place tomorrow to pick up the cash. If it ain't there, you're a dead man!" Satan is left with nothing to say but, "Okay, Okay, I understand."

See questions

7 8 34 40

Pick of the Weak...Not!

There's nothing more important for the budding Eric Clapton than a cool-looking guitar pick. Make the wrong choice, and you can kiss your career goodbye.

Enter Tokyo's Banpresto. That fine purveyor of essential plastic things has taken the innocuous pick and fused it with Super Saiyan power.

After the success of Lupin III and Mobile Suit Gundam comes 20 sets of picks decorated with the coolest designs from the DBZ series. With Dragon Ball Z in your fingers, no longer will your guitar efforts sound like Sid Vicious sober! Simply select the $3.50 pair that suits your musical tastes and watch the record contracts come pouring in.

And if your overly picky about your picks, then choose one of four sets simply labeled "secret." With these, you've absolutely no idea what you'll get until you've handed over your cash. Life just keeps getting better.

Take your pick: A choice selection of DBZ guitar picks
http://www.banpresto.co.jp/

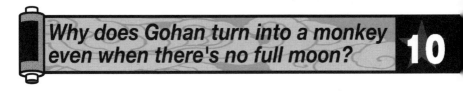

Why does Gohan turn into a monkey even when there's no full moon? **10**

When Goku and Vegeta are slugging it out in a fight to the death, Vegeta hopes to win by changing into a giant monkey. He looks for the moon, but can't find it anywhere. "It's not there! There's no moon! Where the hell has it gone?! Damn that guy, everything he does makes me mad! He went and extinguished the moon before they could even shout, 'Let's get ready to rumble!'"

Kaio is looking down from the sky, and says to himself, "Listen up Saiyan! No matter how hard you try to find it, it's just not there. The moon has gone!"

But Vegeta shouts to Goku, "So, it's you that's gone and knocked out the moon, eh? Well, I'm not going to let that happen! I'll tell you why I change when I see the moon. You know that moonlight is just the reflection from the sun, right?! When that light is reflected off the moon, it contains Brutz Waves! The power of those Brutz Waves tops 17 million zenos at the time of the full moon. When I filter those

See Glossary

Full Moon

47

17 million zenos through my eyes, it sets off a reaction in my tail and I begin to change! Sure, there are plenty of planets in space that have moons, but no matter how big they are, they don't give off 17 million zenos at any other time than when they're full."

While there is no full moon orbiting Earth at that point, Vegeta explains, "There are a few Saiyans who can artificially produce a mini full moon using the oxygen on the moon and this power ball!"

And Vegeta ups and produces a full moon, after which, he changes into a giant monkey! Goku looks as if he's had it, but summons up the last of his strength to release the Genkidama to knock Vegeta out. But the Genkidama misses Vegeta. Instead, the light rays hit Gohan, changing him into a giant monkey!

What Vegeta says about producing a mini full moon using its oxygen and his power ball is true. In fact, Goku is also able to conjure up such a moon, meaning he has no difficulty changing into a giant monkey.

In the 21st Tournament, Goku does just that and goes beserk, forcing Master Roshi to destroy the moon with his Kamehameha.

See Glossary

Genkidama

See questions

7 17 18

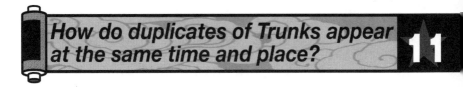

How do duplicates of Trunks appear at the same time and place?

11

We've all seen time machines in Sci-Fi movies or read about them in novels. As the name suggests, they're machines for traveling to the past and future. However, what is often not made clear is the phenomenon known as "time paradox." An example of time paradox is when someone from the future meets himself in the past. In such a case, that person would be duplicated in the same time and place!

Of course, this is something that should never happen. There are so many problems that could occur if someone met his or her self in another dimension. Indeed, there is the danger of altering the future and even destroying the world.

In Dragon Ball Z, Trunks goes back and meets himself as a baby. However, there is no suggestion in the storyline that he disappears or that anything harmful happens to him.

However, according to Trunks, the future that he comes from and the world of Dragon

Ball are slightly different. Which means that each time Trunks goes off time traveling, a new future is established.

The future that Trunks comes from is in the midst of havoc wreaked by Android 17 and 18, who are out to destroy the world. However, they have yet to kill anyone in the present world. In fact, Android 18 even becomes Kuririn's wife!

In Dragon Ball, it's possible to actually come from the future and meet yourself in past. But all this coming and going in time creates thousands of parallel worlds, and nobody really knows how many there are and what they all mean!

See Glossary

Android

See questions

28 39 40

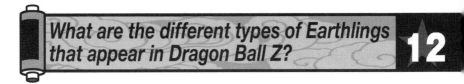

What are the different types of Earthlings that appear in Dragon Ball Z?

12

I n the world of Dragon Ball Z, it's possible to meet many kinds of Earthlings who are different to what are normally considered "human beings." A case in point is the dog king who rules the kingdom. Do we refer to him as a member of the canine race, or do we call him an animal-type human?

Then there is Oolong the pig, Puar, who looks like a cat, Toninjinka, the boss of the Rabbit Army, and a werewolf who takes part in the Tenkaichi Tournament. They all look like animals, but walk on two legs and speak like humans.

Some, like Oolong and Puar, can change into different shapes and forms. Others are less fortunate. The werewolf has no chance of changing back into a human being since Master Roshi blasted the moon away with his Kamehameha during the 21st Tournament!

Indeed, he gives Roshi a piece of his mind when they meet at the 22nd Tournament, saying, "Thanks to you, I've got to walk around

See Glossary
King
Rabbit Army
Tenkaichi Tournament

looking like a werewolf for the rest of my life! No way any cute Earthling chick will even look at me!" But in the end, Roshi hypnotizes the werewolf, allowing him to change back into a human being.

The werewolf's unwholesome looks are part of his charm, but given that he changes with the moon, it may be more accurate to classify him as a specter than as an animal.

As for other creatures that don't exist in the real world, there is the mermaid that Goku digs up and brings along when Roshi says he will allow him to train under his tutelage only if he brings "a sweet, sexy young thing!" She's certainly cute, but should be more accurately regarded as a sprite.

Then there are the actual humans, such as Buruma, Chi-Chi, Yamcha and Kuririn. These guys have no special powers and are considered to be normal people.

Other, stranger characters exist, such as Lunch, who undergoes a Jekyll-and-Hyde character change every time she sneezes; Chaozu, who has supernatural powers; and Tenshinhan, who has three eyes!

And let's not forget that Kuririn has no nose! This isn't because the author Akira Toriyama was unable to draw it in, but because it never existed in the first place! Not having a nose helps Kuririn in the 21st Tenkaichi Tournament when he faces off against the unwashed smelly Bacterian. That's because he doesn't have to experience Bacterian's foul odor.

Even among the humans there are those who seem just like us but are advanced-types, or mutants. While they may look like human beings, they are very different. Two such characters are 300-year-old Roshi, with his exceptional fighting powers, and his elder sister, the fortuneteller Uranai Baba, who can call the dead back to life but only for a day.

Finally, there are the monsters, such as Pilaf. This type, which originates in devildom and Hell, is seldom seen among the Earthlings. Giran, who takes part in the 21st Tournament, has all the appearances of a monster, but then he pops up speaking just like a human being when he shouts, "I'll get you, you little squirt!"

See questions

1 4 9 13
23 24 30 31

Dragon Ball Collection Vol.1
Oolong
$2.00

DBZ File 004

Cell on the Cell

Ever felt the urge to have Goku and friends dangling around your ear while you're on the phone? I know I have. Well now you can, thanks to the wonderful people at Banpresto.

Okay, okay, so DBZ phone straps are nothing new (unless you live in Ohio). But what makes these puppies so special is that each one comes weighed down with not one, but three characters and all seven dragon balls!

Presented in cool DBZ boxes are Freeza, Gohan and Goku or Vegeta, Trunks and Cell, plus a Dragon Ball cell phone strap, plus an interchangeable plate strap. Don't know which one to buy? Then get them both!

Hanging on the Telephone
$11.50
http://www.banpresto.co.jp/

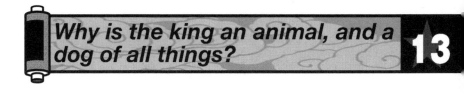

Why is the king an animal, and a dog of all things?

13

The Dragon Ball Z world is one country or nation, divided into 43 regions and ruled by a king. Even though this king may look like an animal, all is not what it seems, as he is in fact human.

There is no explanation as to what kind of life he led before becoming king, but from the many speeches he makes each time Earth looks set to be destroyed, we can see that he has a very strong sense of justice.

For example, he is urged by his followers to evacuate when Piccolo comes to blows with Goku, but hesitates as his sense of responsibility will not allow the king to flee while his subjects are fighting.

Unfortunately, his police force is weak, meaning he is unable to control the country on his own. So no matter how good his intentions are, he lacks an ability to get things done.

We must not overlook what Buruma says at the start of the story: "It seems that the person who collected all the dragon balls became

See Glossary

King

king." This is how it "seems," but the explanation never gets beyond the realm of supposition, and we should remember that Buruma herself was a mere child when she said this.

We can't totally rule out what she says, but at the same time we shouldn't accept it as fact. Like when she explains her reason for searching for the dragon balls: "I know what my wish will be! I was so much looking forward to picking more strawberries than I could possibly eat, but what I really want is my prince charming!"

See questions

1 2 12 13
20 27

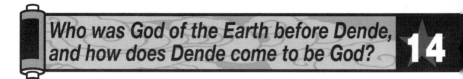

Who was God of the Earth before Dende, and how does Dende come to be God?

14

Dende is selected to be the new Kamisama, the God of the Earth. There hasn't been a Kamisama for some time, and the previous Kami looked exactly like Piccolo.

Piccolo was also a Namek, who escaped in a spaceship and came to Earth when Planet Namek's climate began to change. We know from the words of Mr. Popo, servant to the future Kamisama, what it was like for the still young Kami to come to Earth and what he did there.

"It was about 100 years ago. Kamisama told Mr. Popo about his past. Very unusual thing for a Kamisama to do. Very strange tale. Kamisama said he lived on the Yunzabit heights. So, Mr. Popo asked, Yunzabit way out on the edge. No place for people to live. So, why were you there? Kamisama said he didn't know why he was in such a place. Said he bumped his head and lost his memory."

According to what Kamisama tells Goku,

See Glossary

Planet Namek

Mr. Popo

this is what happened, "Long ago, Piccolo and I were one...There was a genius martial arts expert...He heard about Kamisama and came here...Just like you. But sad to say, Kamisama died...I wanted to be his successor...But no matter how long I waited, I was never recognized... Even though I believed there was no one else better than I...It was because in the depths of my heart resided the barest scintilla of evil...Kamisama had seen it, and knew it....I was able to dispel the evil after extreme training...That evil was Piccolo Daimao... I became the new Kamisama, but he escaped to Earth and terrorized the inhabitants of the planet...I feel a great responsibility for that."

In other words, about 300 hundred years ago, Kamisama was able to dispel the evil within him by undergoing a regimen of hard training. Because of this, he was recognized by the previous Kamisama and became his successor.

But what is difficult to understand is how, after the previous Kamisama rose to the position only after great hardship, does Dende - Namek though he may be - become the next Kamisama with so much ease. Perhaps it is because, after spending time with Earthlings such as Goten and Kuririn, Dende's heart is left pure and his mind clear.

See questions

27 47

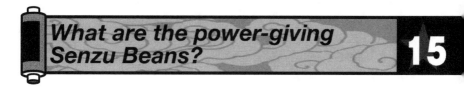

What are the power-giving Senzu Beans?

15

Senzu Beans are grown at Karin's Tower. They are known for their power-enhancing qualities and their ability to stave off hunger for at least ten days at a time.

No matter how beaten up the body is, after just one bean, everything clicks back into place. A single bean will fill most stomachs, though big eaters such as Yajirobe can eat a lot of them.

Karin's jar once held many such beans, but they disappear one after another during the fierce fighting that unfolds. Goku, Kuririn and Gohan take the last two beans, with Goku eating one whole bean and Kuririn and Gohan eating half each ahead of their fight with Vegeta and Nappa.

Goku suffers an almost fatal wound in his fight with Vegeta, and in hospital afterwards is feeling sorry for himself, saying, "What a bummer. Four months to recover, and I might never be the same again."

But Karin, who has come to visit him,

See Glossary

Karin's Tower

cheers him up by saying, "No cause for concern. The new beans will on the trees in a month!" From this we realize that the precious beans grow on trees, but there is never any specific explanation made for their amazing powers.

See questions
29

When was the ki energy first felt? 16

At the start of the story, no one uses the term "*ki* energy." The first one to experience it is Goku. While participating in the 23rd Tenkaichi Tournament, Goku spits out the words, "So, Piccolo Daimao has reared his ugly head has he..." when he senses that Piccolo (Majunior) is in the arena.

Then, five years later, when the Saiyan Raditz attacks Earth, it's Piccolo who is able to sense his coming when he says, "Just what is this awful power that is approaching..."

Goku feels it too, saying, "God, what incredible power...! Just what the hell is it...!?" Kuririn, on the other hand, can't feel a thing. Still, even while Goku and Piccolo are able sense the *ki*, they are not able to understand where the power is emanating from or its strength.

One year later, when Vegeta and Nappa come to Earth, Piccolo, Gohan, Yamcha, Kuririn, Yajirobe, Tenshinhan and Chaozu are all able to feel the power simultaneously. And

See Glossary
Tenkaichi Tournament

that's despite the fact that the two have landed far away to the east.

They all know of the attack by the Saiyans beforehand because of the training they do to heighten their fighting strengths. This probably leads them to being able to feel the *ki* energy.

The Saiyans, on the other hand, are equipped with the Scouter, enabling them to determine the fighting capabilities of their opponents.

When Vegeta faces off against Freeza's henchmen Zarbon on Namek, he says, "Me... I'm going to Earth... those guys down there, they have a way of figuring out an opponent's strength and where he is without using no damned Scouter. It's just so easy once you know how. You guys'll never figure it out, especially if, like Freeza, all you do is try and work out how powerful a guy is..."

See Glossary
Scouter

See questions

3 5 16 17
18 23 24 25
26 27 31

Fan Forum

Ring Name: Peking Duck
Years on Earth: ?
DBZ Origin: 1987
Dragon Net: http://duck.cool.ne.jp/

cocoro books: How did you first get into Dragon Ball?
Peking Duck: I really liked the episode where Goku comes back to Earth to fight in the 23rd Tenkaichi Tournament. One week he's still a kid and the next week he's suddenly all grown up! I remember reading that week's Shonen Jump over and over again.

cb: Out of all the Dragon Ball anime, manga and movies, what's your favorite scene?
PD: The coolest scene is in the anime when Gohan becomes super powerful after witnessing Cell showing off after trampling Android 16. I thought the actual images were amazing, and the background music, which was called Lucky Day (Unmei no Hi), was perfect. That was the best!

cb: You've got a huge collection of Dragon Ball stuff! When did you start collecting? And why?
PD: I first started collecting the character cards Carddas about 15 years ago. At that time, every Japanese kid was mad about trading cards. But because I was at junior high, I was a bit embarrassed about buying those cards. Carddas were only sold from vending machines, and I used to save all the 100-yen coins I got and go and buy loads of them. I didn't realize, but some of the local kids used to watch me, and I felt a bit stupid when I found out.

After that I started collecting Dragon Ball stationery and then got into toys.

cb: How big is your collection? And how much did it all cost?

PD: I've never really counted everything, but if I don't include the cards, there's probably about 1500 to 2000 items. I don't want to even think about how many cards I've got. There's got to be more than 30,000! The whole lot probably cost more than 10,000 dollars!

cb: What are some of your favorite pieces?

PD: Easily, the best thing I've got is the Complete Dragon Ball set of ten books. It's the whole Dragon Ball series in one set - a must-have for DB fans. I've never found any other books that have so much DB info. It's amazing!

My second favorite thing is an autographed lithograph by Akira Toriyama. It's from a collection of some 200 works by the artist that were exhibited across Japan. Toriyama signed it with an ink brush.

Complete Dragon Ball Set

Next, I like my collection of Dragon Ball hit music. I've got all 18 albums, but the one I like best is #14, Adventure in the Sky (Sora wo Meguru Boken). Dragon Ball's got this sort of action-packed violent image, but this music's really soothing. The other albums have got a lot of the famous songs on them, many of them have been used as BGM.

Toriyama's Autographed Lithograph

Dragon Ball Z Hits Series

cb: What are your best three rare items?

PD: Number 1 is a cutout of DBZ Super Butouden 2. It was used as a store display. I talked with the staff there and finally they let me have it. These things usually get thrown away, so it's really rare.

Number 2 is a McDonald's Dragon Ball menu. When *The Road to the Strongest* came out in 1996, there was a tie-up with MacDonald's, and they sold these meals called Happy Sets. I asked the manager if I could get one of the menu panels. I doubt many collectors have got one.

Number 3 is Playdia Dragon Ball Z. These are really hard to get now. It's a Bandai computer game and software. It uses a lot of the original Dragon Ball animation, so it's really cool to watch. They're not made anymore, so you'll have a hard time finding one now.

McDonald's Dragon Ball Menu

DBZ Super Butouden
2 Cutout

Playdia Dragon Ball Z

cb: What are some of the problems you've had as a collector?

PD: Getting hold of stuff that's not for sale can be hard, like things used for advertising. Stores tend to throw posters and POPs away once they've been used. I always think that if I don't get hold of something it's going to disappear forever.

The McDonald's Happy Set is a good example. At that time I was at university, and everyday for about three weeks I went to McDonalds and ordered two sets. They were meant for kids, so it was a bit embarrassing, but I managed to get all the toys that came with them. On the last day of the campaign, I asked the manager for a menu, and he gave me one.

cb: What is it about Dragon Ball that you like so much?

PD: I like the characters, and I like how much fun they all are. Once you know each individual character, you realize that they're all great. And I think that they're drawn really well. I just have to look at the pictures, and I feel good.

cb: What makes you happy?

PD: When I can talk about Dragon Ball with other fans, I guess. I mean, I love watching the anime and drawing my own DBZ manga, but the best feeling is hanging out with other fans. I'm so glad there are loads of fans!

Peking Duck's Three Fave DBZ Characters

1. Son Goku

He's always so happy and full of life. When I look at him, it makes me feel good.

2. Vegeta

I like the fact that he's so proud and self-controlled.

by Peking Duck

3. Buruma

Being a guy, I obviously like her when she dressed up as a Bunny Girl.

Peking Duck's Fave Collectibles

Mini Painting Book
The DBZ story develops so fast, that there's always a new painting book coming out. There are 53 of them so far.

Koizumi Desk POPs
I begged this furniture company to give me some of their DB POPS.

DBZ Super Shampoo
Every year the company brings out a new design. There are three different types.

Dragon Ball GT Curry
I've had this so long that it's passed its sell-by date.

Kids' Shoes

Dragon Ball GT Stationery Set

Dragon Ball Hits Set

Children's Eye-drops
These are sold in the summer, when kids use the pool. They come with a little holder. Each year the company brings out two or three different styles.

Disposable Hot Pads
Every year there's a new design.

Swimming Float
This is a real rare item.

Bingo Card

68

Family, Friends and Nauseous Foes

Dragon Ball Collection Vol.1
Goku
$2.00

Is Goku an Earthling? 17

Although Goku believes himself to be an Earthling, others are doubtful about this because he isn't anything like the humans they know. For one, he has a tail. And then there's his habit of changing into a huge monkey every time he sees a full moon.

Raditz the Saiyan, who comes from space and, unknown to Goku, is his elder brother, is quite sure Goku is not from Earth. "You are not from this planet," he tells Goku matter-of-factly.

Goku is, in fact, a Saiyan - his real name being Kakarot. Saiyans are known as a war-loving, bellicose race that go around annihilating the inhabitants of planets with benign atmospheres and selling the planets off to other aliens at inflated prices.

Goku was sent to Earth as a baby with the mission to wipe out all life on the planet. However, he falls into a valley and loses his memory. He is raised as a human by foster parents, and is taught that people are good.

See Glossary
Goku's Tail
Full moon

So, when he changes into a gigantic monkey, he is really only reverting to his former Saiyan self - doing what any normal Saiyan would do.

It's also true that the same warrior blood that runs through Saiyan veins is in Goku as well. No matter how strong an opponent he faces, it's part of Goku's psychological make-up to relish the chance for a fresh fight.

However, while the Saiyans go around methodically wiping out the populations of entire planets, there is an extremely compassionate side to Goku's character, as shown in the way he protects Earth until the very end. In that sense, maybe we can call him a "Saiyan Earthling." In fact, he probably values peace and friendship more than the average Earthling.

See questions

10 18 19

Who are the Saiyans? 18

Raditz, Goku's elder brother, gives a good explanation of what Saiyans are when he announces after his arrival on Earth, "I am a Saiyan, a member of the proudest and strongest warrior tribe in all space."

Goku is also a Saiyan. According to Master Roshi, "Long ago, the late Son Gohan told me that he picked up this baby that had a tail, but he was a wild little thing who wouldn't take to me no matter what I did. God, he was difficult. Anyway, one day he trips and falls into a valley, hitting his head, and we all think he's gonna die. But this kid has some kind of incredible life force in him, and survives. And to top it off, afterwards he turns into a sweet little child. Who would 'a thunk it?!"

Goku's Saiyan name - his real name - is Kakarot and, according to Raditz, "He was sent here with the expressed purpose of ridding the planet of you damned human beings!"

Saiyans are the invaders and real estate sharks of the universe. Their basic mission is to find planets, annihilate the inhabitants, and sell them off at a profit.

The Saiyans closely mirror elements of organized crime in the '80s, which took advantage of Japan's asset bubble to drive residents off prime real estate and sell it off at vast profits.

However, they have a sad history behind them. They were originally a minority on their home planet of Vegeta. When the planet was hit by a gigantic meteorite and imploded, almost all Saiyans disappeared into the sands of space, leaving only four survivors, including Goku. Knowing this, it's difficult to understand what Raditz is thinking when he tries to kill Goku. He is, in turn, killed by Piccolo.

One year after this event, Vegeta and Nappa attack Earth. Nappa loses to Goku and his Kaioken, suffering a near mortal wound. The proud Vegeta will not accept the fact that Nappa has lost to Goku, who he considers to be an inferior warrior, and subsequently destroys Nappa with his own hands.

This means that before the birth of Gohan, Goten and Trunks, there are only two surviving Saiyans, Goku and Vegeta.

See Glossary

Planet Vegeta
Kaioken

See questions

4 16 17 25
26 27 28 32

Does Goku have innocent blood on his hands?

19

Tragic, but a fact of the Dragon Ball story is that Goku is responsible for the death of an innocent person. However, having said that, there is a reason for it.

Goku was born a Saiyan on Planet Vegeta, where his name was Kakarot. Before Vegeta was hit by a gigantic meteorite and destroyed, Goku was sent to Earth as a baby with the purpose of wiping out all living creatures on the face of the planet. However, he falls into a valley and loses his memory. This is when he is found by Son Gohan, a follower of Master Roshi, and raised as the human, Son Goku.

As well as teaching Goku martial arts, Roshi raises him to live as a human being. Thanks to Roshi, Goku grows up to be rather a naive kid with the kindest of feelings.

Goku loves Gohan, and the extent of his feelings can be seen when he fights Gohan, who has been brought back to life for a single day in order to have Uranai Baba reveal the location of the dragon balls. When Goku real-

See Glossary

Planet Vegeta

izes whom he is fighting, tears well up in his eyes and he shouts for joy, "Granddad, Granddad, Granddad!"

Buruma remarks that "I didn't think I would ever see Goku cry." But Yamcha looks fondly at Goku and replies, "Not unusual in the least. I mean, no matter how strong he may be, he's still a kid." Puar also starts crying when she sees Goku's tears.

During the fight, Gohan attempts to force Goku to overcome his one weakness by grabbing his tail. When the fight is over, Gohan and Roshi talk in whispers so as not to be overheard by Goku. "And he won't just up and turn into a gigantic monkey, then?" "Fear not, he's been as right as rain since I blasted the moon away."

This conversation reveals the secret that Granddad Gohan takes with him to the grave. Goku's tail is a unique Saiyan feature, and while being a weak point, it is also the medium through which he changes into a giant monkey when he sees the moon. Without their tails, Saiyans cannot turn into monkeys, and if the tail is removed, even after becoming monkeys, they revert to their original forms.

When Goku fights Vegeta, the latter says, "Shall I tell you something? When Saiyans change into gigantic monkeys, their fighting

See Glossary

Goku's Tail

powers are multiplied by ten!"

Hearing this, Goku recalls Gohan telling him, "Goku, on full moon nights, the giant monkey, the bogeyman, comes out. So whatever you do, you must not leave the house. Everything will be just fine if you stay sound asleep." He also remembers Kamisama saying, "Shall I fix it so your tail disappears for ever? It must get in the way."

Goku finally realizes: "Now I see it. God! So, that thing which stomped Granddad to death, and appeared at the Tenkaichi Tournament and smashed the place up... that was me!" Then, deep from within his heart, he exclaims, "Sorry Granddad! You were really something. I probably wouldn't have had a chance of beating you unless I used up all my natural powers. Now you're dead and gone. I don't know how I could ever begin to apologize to you even if you were here again."

When Goku changes into the gigantic monkey he is still Goku...and yet he is not Goku! He loses his memory and has no idea what is being said. Therefore, when he stomped all over his Granddad, it was an accident, and in one sense, Goku is not to blame.

Evidence of this can be seen in the fact that not only does Gohan not blame Goku, he also tries to avoid Goku finding out what hap-

See Glossary

Full moon

pened, so as to prevent him from suffering with guilt.

When Goku dies while fighting his elder brother Raditz, even Enma Daio doesn't condemn Goku for killing Gohan. "Ah, let me see now...Son Goku, you say...Yes, yes, you have a wonderful record."

Goku may be responsible for Gohan's death, but it was an accident, and Goku bears no blame. Even Enma Daio agrees on that.

See questions

2 10 17 18
20 23 25 45

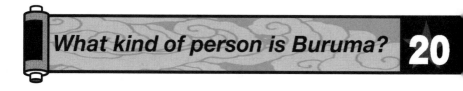

What kind of person is Buruma? 20

uruma is there right at the start of the tale. As well as being the next person to appear after the main character, Goku, she's the first girl that we meet. She's also looking for the dragon balls to help in her search for her "Prince Charming." Buruma plays a very important role in the story.

By her appearance, she comes across as a little cutesy. But she is, in fact, a no-nonsense straight-talker. This we quickly learn when she calls Goku a "country hick!" and tells him "no hanky-panky!" and "You have to learn how to be nice to girls." She's also quite prepared to flash her panties - even though no one has asked her to - if it gets her closer to the dragon balls.

We could be nice about her and call her down-to-earth, except that she has the habit of saying the first thing that comes into her head. She's also a sucker for good-looking guys. After all, her quest for the dragon balls is based on her pinning down Mr. Right - who must be handsome.

When Yamcha first appears, it's as a baddie stealing from people who have become lost and wandered into the wasteland. He even threatens Goku, "Hand over yer' capsules and yer' cash!" Still, Buruma ends up falling in love with Yamcha.

As has been described, she thinks nothing of flashing her panties to get what she wants, and judges men only by their looks. With the character of Buruma, the author may have been looking to satirize today's young Japanese women.

However, while in the real world, Japanese girls are often out for easy money, Buruma is a well brought-up daughter of a rich family and is not after hard cash. This diversion from reality is probably out of consideration for viewers and readers of the manga.

She starts seeing Yamcha, but it doesn't work out. She then has a relationship with Vegeta, and although they don't get married, she gives birth to Trunks. There's no description of her relationship with Vegeta, but it's difficult to imagine she chose him for his looks alone. Now that she's all grown-up, she's probably discovered something deeper than mere appearances.

See questions
2 23 25 28

What is the difference between Kamesenryu and Tsurusenryu? 21

Numerous martial arts exponents and fighting techniques appear in the first part of the story. Among those that make an impression are the Kamesenryu of Kamesennin, Goku's teacher, and the Tsurusenryu of Tsurusennin.

Kamesennin and Tsurusennin were both once pupils of Mutaito, and have been rivals ever since. They are divided over the true approach to martial arts. When they meet, as they escort their own pupils to the Tenkaichi Tournament, they exchange childish insults. "Baldy!" shouts Tsurusennin, to which Kamesennin replies "Half-baked baldy!"

Their teacher Mutaito is the genius martial artist who risked death to trap Piccolo in a pressure cooker using the secret art of Mafuba.

Just as their teacher used *ki* energy, so both Kamesennin and Tsurusennin use such killer techniques like the Kamehameha and Dodonpa that also make use of *ki*.

See Glossary

Tenkaichi Tournament

Mafuba

81

They are both powerful, but while Kamesenryu also encompasses many moves that allow fighters to defeat opponents without resorting to violence, Tsurusenryu is a murderous style. This is evident by the fact that the younger brother of Tsurusenryu - Tao Pai-Pai - is the world's number one killer. In the end, he is killed by Goku.

At the Tenkaichi Tournament, Tsurusennin resorts to foul play to try to defeat Goku, but his pupil Tenshinhan rebels, saying, "I don't want to be a killer anymore!"

As they are based on different approaches, it is difficult to say which school of fighting is the most devastating.

See questions

7 16 22 27

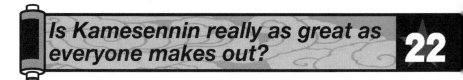

Is Kamesennin really as great as everyone makes out? 22

Kamesennin is a super human, renowned as a god of martial arts and still up to chasing young skirt at 300 years of age. He is also known as Master Roshi (or Muten Roshi) and is famous throughout the fighting world. Gyumao and Son Gohan - Goku's grandfather - were his pupils.

Yet, even though he is recognized as an exceptional person, the first thing he says to Buruma when they meet is, "Show us yer' panties!" She readily complies, only to realize that she isn't wearing any. When she flips up her skirt, the great master is so taken back that his nose starts gushing blood!

But he isn't just some dirty old man who happens to be an expert at martial arts. He is responsible for developing such incredible techniques as the Kamehameha, and is famed for releasing the Mabuha at great risk to himself when Piccolo Daimao is brought back to life thanks to the foolishness of Pilaf.

At the Tenkaichi Tournament that Goku

See Glossary

Mabuha
Tenkaichi Tournament

and Kuririn first participate in, he disguises himself as Jackie Chun and takes part in the memorable bout with Goku. This is not for his own sake, but to keep Goku from forgetting he's still only a student. In other words, the teacher is thinking ahead to the kind of person Goku will become in the future.

While a god of the ring in his own right, Kamesennin is also the first to raise his hat to Goku when he defeats the Red Ribbon Army by himself. He gives Goku the praise he deserves, saying, "It might just be that Goku has grown stronger than me...there is something downright unfathomable about this guy!"

The same overly abundant super powers that probably make Kamesennin such a lecherous old man are also what make him the great person he is. If we forgive his lewdness, we see a man who walks the straight and narrow path of the martial arts master.

See Glossary

Red Ribbon Army

See questions

Is Yamcha's weak point girls? **23**

Yamcha is a bandit of the wastelands, and when he first appears, he threatens Goku, demanding him to "Hand over yer' capsules and yer' cash!" However, when Buruma awakens from her nap, he begins to shake, he stops dead in his tracks, goes bright red and then beats a quick retreat.

"I'm none too sure," he explains, "but I get all kind of tense when women are around. It's not that I don't like 'em...they just make me nervous." Although a thief who never thinks twice about stealing, he's also extremely naive when it comes to the opposite sex.

This is the first impression we have of Yamcha. However, when he later starts seeing Buruma, he cuts his trademark long hair and takes part in the Tenkaichi Tournament. He is transformed, and becomes a remarkably nice young man who trains hard at his martial arts.

Although Yamcha is very strong for a human being, he is surrounded by absolute monsters as fighters, and compared to them,

See Glossary

Tenkaichi Tournament

his fighting record never amounts to much.

His love for Buruma looks set to grow. But later in the story we hear from Trunks, the son of Buruma and Vegeta who arrives from the future, that, "It seems Yamcha is a little bit fickle when it comes to women, and that he split up with Buruma after a fight."

It is not explained in as many words, but it's ironic that the naive bandit who dreamed of marriage becomes careless in his attitude to women after cleaning himself up and becoming a law-abiding citizen. This may, after all, have become his weak point.

See questions

7 20 28

Dragon Ball Collection Vol.1
Yamcha
$2.00

What kind of person is Kuririn? 24

Kuririn turns up just as Kamesennin lands Goku with the ridiculous initiation test of bringing him a nice, ripe young girl.

When Kuririn asks Kamesennin to accept him as a pupil, the teacher turns him down flat, saying "Tough kiddo, but I hardly ever accept pupils. Just forget it." So, without batting an eyelid, Kuririn hands Kamesennin a girly mag. Kamesennin is suddenly persuaded. "Well, I'll think about it," he say.

Kuririn isn't shy about telling people that the reason he wants to train under Kamesennin and become a martial arts expert is to get closer to girls. It also seems he was bullied by the older boys when he was at Tarin Temple.

However, Kuririn has absolutely no time for romance once he begins the strict training regime. Instead, he fights against one strong opponent after another, although he does find time to sneak off once in while to find something to eat.

The relationship between Kuririn and Goku truly starts to develop when they begin taking on their adversaries. Kuririn becomes Goku best friend and, in Dragon Ball, Kuririn is the toughest of all the humans.

The first time he falls in love, it is with the beautiful Android 18. Instead of exchanging formal greetings, she kisses him on the cheek, causing him to flip out. Kuririn reciprocates by calling on Shenlong to remove the bomb that's inside her body. However, even with this, she continues to treat him with disdain. "Don't get any funny ideas, dummy," she tells him. Eventually, she falls for his kindness, and they get married. They have a cute little girl called Maron and make a warm and loving home.

See Glossary
Android
Maron

See questions

2 4 9 12
22 40

Why is Vegeta such a cold, hard creature?

25

Vegeta is a warrior Saiyan prince with superior fighting skills and an over-abundance of pride. It's not so much a case of Vegeta alone being cold and aloof, but that Saiyans themselves are a hard, calculating race. Let's not forget that Raditz, the elder brother of Goku, has the same cold, calculating characteristics. Or, until he banged his head, Goku himself was violent.

For Vegeta, fighting is the purpose of life, and he is always looking to reemerge stronger than everyone else. When he first comes to Earth, it's in the spirit of vengeance. He thinks nothing of Goku. "Goku is a traitor to all of us Saiyans, and like all traitors, he will be dealt with severely...I will kill his son and his friends while he watches, then I will make him suffer long and hard, making him see how powerless he is in the face of my onslaught, before allowing him to die."

When Nappa, who comes to Earth with Vegeta, is defeated by Goku thanks to his training with Kaio, Vegeta rails, "I have no need for Saiyans who can do nothing! Die!" and he blasts Nappa to bits. For Vegeta to lose is to incur shame, and his terrible pride dictates that he must kill his kinsman rather than suffer the shame of defeat.

However, even the cold, heartless, war-loving Vegeta is forced to give Goku his due after witnessing him in battle after battle. When Goku dies at the hands of Cell, Vegeta pours out scorn and frustration at not having being able to beat him himself when he says, "Damned Kakarot. What a way to die!"

While there is something perverse in what he says, it's also an expression of his recognition that Goku is his major rival. And slowly but surely something changes within him. While he fights without any show of emotion, when he sees his son, Trunks, killed by Cell, he lets out a scream, "Aargh, no!" and leaps on Cell with murder in his eyes.

At the end of the story, he finally shows that he's able to recognize others when he says, "Go for it Kakarot! you're the best!"

See Glossary

"Go for it Kakarot! You're the best!"

See questions

4 18 28 33

DBZ File 006

Dragon Ball Who's Who

Every character in Dragon Ball Z seems to have a weird or funny name. Some are English, like Trunks and Lunch. But most are invented names that work as puns in the original Japanese. Once you know the meanings of these names, it's not only possible to get a deeper understanding of the individual characters, but also to get some insight into the mind of Dragon Ball creator, Akira Toriyama (whose family name means Bird Mountain, by the way).

Names from Food

Zabon	A large citrus fruit
Gohan	Steamed rice
Kuririn	From *kuri*, a chestnut
Chaba	Tealeaf
Nappa	Rape leaves, or vegetables served in a meal; greens
Saiyan	In Japanese "saiya-jin." In reverse, "yasai," meaning "vegetable"
Ebi-furiya	Fried shrimp in Japan is known as "ebi-furai." However, in Nagoya, where Toriyama is from, it is pronounced "ebi-furiya"
Udo	A mountain plant with white edible leaves. Also means a "good-for-nothing"
Kishime	From *kishimen*, a type of noodle
Zakro	From *zakuro*, a pomegranate
Jagger Batta Danshaku	Hot potatoes with butter. "Danshaku" is a potato type
Shamo	A type of chicken favored for its meat and eggs
Sansho	Pepper
Daiz	*Daizu*, soybeans
Dr. Wheelo	*Uiro*, a cookie made from rice flower, sugar and flavoring. It is a Nagoya specialty.
Dr. Kochin	*Kochin* is a type of chicken eaten in Nagoya.
Tanmen	A type of *ramen*
Bongo	From "bongore," the Japanese pronunciation of "vongole," a spaghetti dish
Rakase	From *rakkasei*, peanuts

Names from Animals

Katattsu	From *katatsumuri,* or snail
Dende	From *dendenmushi*, another word for "snail"
Namek	From *namekuji*, a slug
Zunama	From *namazu*, a catfish
Bihe	From *hebi*, a snake

Other Names

Akuman	From *akuma*, the Devil
Gokua	From *gokuaku*, meaning "atrocious""
Chi-Chi	Mother's or cow's milk
Dr. Gero	Gero means "vomit"
Otokosuki	Homosexual
Idasa	From *dasai*, unfashionable; uncool
Ikose	From *sekoi*, stingy; tightfisted
Muri	Impossible
Mokekko	From *mo kekko*, meaning "It's enough;" "No more thank you"
Okkane Mane	From *okane*, money
Gyosan Mane	From *gyosan*, in Kansai dialect means "much;" "a lot." Means "much money"
Zangya	From *zangyaku*, cruel

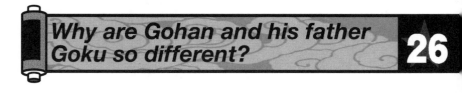

Why are Gohan and his father Goku so different? 26

Gohan has such a gentle way about him, even though his father is a warrior Saiyan. His mother, Chi-Chi, is set on her son getting a good education and, even when still small, he says such things as, "I want to be a scholar." (And that is what he becomes in the end.)

Although Goku loves fighting, he would never do anything to hurt anyone other than the real baddies. And as for the differences in their characters, let's not forget that Goku came alone as a baby from Planet Vegeta and was raised by the martial arts sensei Son Gohan. Gohan, on the other hand, is brought up by Chi-Chi almost single-handedly, as Goku's exploits in the fighting world often keep him away from home. That's probably one reason for the difference in their respective characters.

Goku dies in the fight with Raditz, leaving Gohan in the hands of the Namek Piccolo, who must train him in preparation for the next

See Glossary

Planet Vegeta

Saiyan invasion. They somehow manage to fight back Vegeta, but Piccolo dies defending Gohan. When the Saiyans will invade again, nobody knows.

Without Piccolo, there are no dragon balls. So, Gohan decides he must travel to Namek, Piccolo's home planet. But he meets with fierce opposition from Chi-Chi, as he'll fall behind in his studies if he takes such a long trip. Goku is furious with his mother. "This is no time to be saying anything like that! We are all fighting to save the earth and bring back to life those who have died. We must fight the Saiyans," he tells her.

With this, we can see that he is a man of high principles like his father, but at the same time he has common sense and is more easily able to adapt to the society around him.

See questions

2 7 17 18
25 27

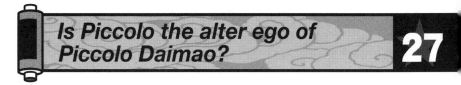

Is Piccolo the alter ego of Piccolo Daimao?

27

Piccolo Daimao, the Demon King, seizes King's Castle and sets out to take over Earth through terror and evil. His plans are curtailed when he's imprisoned in the Denshi Jar, but he eventually frees himself and looks set to wreak more havoc. However, two days later, he is brought down by Son Goku. About to die, Piccolo Daimao spits out an egg containing a genetic duplicate of himself - Majunior, the current Piccolo.

Piccolo Daimao entrusts his last wishes to the egg - "My child, avenge your father's death...You must plant the seeds of evil."

When the new Piccolo hatches out, he too burns with the same evil desires, wanting nothing more than to confront Goku and destroy him.

Everyone believes Piccolo to be Piccolo Daimao reborn. But in truth, their characters are very different.

While Piccolo Daimao is boundlessly cruel, Piccolo doesn't kill without reason, shift-

See Glossary

"My child, avenge your father's death...You must plant the seeds of evil."

ing toward goodness and away from evil as he grows older. While he is clearly the child of Daimao, the two are not the same.

Before he takes on his most powerful adversary, Cell, he powers up by fusing with Kamisama, who is also a Namek. Indeed, they were originally a single being.

It's also Piccolo who trains Gohan in preparation for the next Saiyan invasion. He even becomes fond of Gohan when he sees him persevering in his training as he struggles to overcome his weaknesses.

This growing affection is what drives Piccolo to make the ultimate sacrifice. During the fight with Nappa and Vegeta, Piccolo throws himself in front of Gohan to shield him from a shock wave, and as a result, he dies, uttering his last tearful words, "Those few months we spent together? They weren't bad kiddo." I'm dying Gohan..."

See Glossary

"Those few months we spent together? They weren't bad kiddo."

See questions

26 33

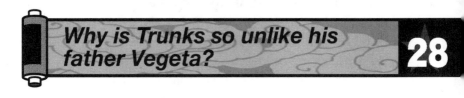

Why is Trunks so unlike his father Vegeta?

28

Many of the repugnant elements of Vegeta's personality can be blamed on the fact that he's a Saiyan. Trunks may be the son of Vegeta, but he's also half human - his mother is Buruma. Because of this human side, Trunks and his father come across as very different individuals.

The grown-up Trunks arrives from 20 years in the future to save Earth. As he tells Goku, "In the fights three years from now, my father, Kuririn, Yamcha, Tenshinhan, Chaozu and even Piccolo are all killed. Only Gohan manages to survive. He becomes my master, teaching me all I know, but even he died four years ago. And you know, with the death of Piccolo, the dragon balls disappear and it's no longer possible to bring anyone back to life. The future where I live has become a living hell thanks to the androids, who take their time and pleasure in slowly but surely wiping out all life."

Trunk's father, Vegeta, also dies before Trunks is old enough to remember very much.

See Glossary

Android

So, to save the earth, Trunks boards the time machine that his mother has worked so hard to make and returns to 20 years past.

It is then that he meets his father for the first time. "I was so happy to meet him," Trunks exclaims. But the two are soon at loggerheads when they come up against the androids.

After Vegeta announces, "I want this one for myself, here and now. The fight with that last android was a waste of time!" Trunks tells him, "You mustn't say that. You overlook the power of the androids. We should find the labs where they're made and destroy them before they can begin to function, just as Piccolo did. And if we can't do that right away, then we should wait until Goku recovers."

Either because of the hardships of the world he inhabits, or because of the way his mother has raised him, Trunks is already a well-developed person even before he reaches manhood - quite the opposite of his egoist father.

But he remains the son of Vegeta, and because of this his strength is phenomenal and he can freely change into a Saiyan. Even Trunks the child - not Future Trunks - shows the instinctive Saiyan appetite for fighting at the Tenkaichi Tournaments.

See Glossary
Tenkaichi Tournament

See questions

2 7 11 18
20 23 24 25
26 27 31 35
40

Is Yajirobe just a glutton who spends all his time pigging out? 29

Goku awakes, weak and hungry after being beaten senseless by Tambourine, and goes off in search of food. He finally comes across a huge fish cooking over a fire. Thinking that it's been forgotten by somebody, he tucks in and soon has eaten the lot.

But then a rock comes flying out of nowhere at Goku. He looks up to see a long-haired, fat kid. This is Yajirobe, the fish was his dinner, and he's fuming.

"You scumbag! You stole my fish and ate it on the sly!", he screams.

But Goku had no idea it belonged to anyone. "It was just left there," he says, to which Yajirobe angrily replies, "Idiot! Who would go and leave a fried fish here, there or anywhere?!"

While the two are arguing, Daimao's henchmen Cymbal appears out of the sky, busting for a fight. Yajirobe is willing to accommodate his wishes, and after a punch-up that sees Yajirobe go down, and then come up again, he slices up the monster Cymbal with his sword, cooks up his flesh, and eats it.

By the size of gut, there's no mistaking that Yajirobe likes to eat. Goku is a big eater himself, but Yajirobe takes the cake...literally.

Every being in dragon ball Z is unique. But Yajirobe is surely one of the most unusual. He's not a bad guy in the sense that he wantonly favors evil, but he's certainly got a nasty selfish streak.

When the two first meet, Goku immediately notices the dragon ball hanging around Yajirobe's neck. Yajirobe has no idea of its power, but when Goku asks him for it, he stubbornly refuses to give it up. That is until he realizes he's in trouble when he hears the name of Piccolo Daimao. He immediately hands it to Goku and then runs and hides. Yajirobe's not the kind of guy that anyone would want as a friend.

But he can be persuaded to be of some use if there's food in the offing. When Goku has been beaten almost to death by Piccolo Daimao, he asks Yajirobe to take him to Karin's Tower. Yajirobe obliges, but not before asking, "Sure, I'll take you, but you gotta promise me a good feed for doing so!"

He also comes to Goku's rescue by cutting off Vegeta's tail when they fight.

Yajirobe's too self-centered for his own good. But in the end, it's difficult not to like him.

See Glossary
Tenkaichi Tournament

See questions

2 17

Why does Lunch disappear halfway through the series? 30

In the long-running Dragon Ball series, the development of the story differs entirely between the early and later stages. So too are there are a number of characters who appear in the early parts only to disappear along the way. Lunch is one such character.

Because the story of Dragon Ball is based upon fighting, the characters are predominantly male - although there are plenty of characters that are not human at all!

Even with this in mind, the blue-haired Lunch makes quite an impression. Let's not forget that it was Goku and Kuririn that brought her with them so that she could train under the tutelage of Kamesennin.

When she first arrives, she is beautiful and graceful, although something of a ditz. However, she has a tendency to undergo a Jekyll-and-Hyde transformation each time she sneezes. With this, Lunch changes into Evil Lunch.

Lunch is a sweet, docile girl who is

extremely naive. However, when Lunch sneezes, she becomes an evil, hostile blonde who enjoys killing, robbing and hijacking. To top it all, she is completely unaware of her two-sided character.

When Goku rescues her from the police, she comes to Kame's house, where, the only woman in the group, she flounces around in lingerie. But she is equally attractive after she sneezes and becomes the machinegun-toting, rampaging vixen. Her character probably exists to symbolize womanhood and its duality of character.

However, according to Kuririn, immediately following the 23rd Tenkaichi Tournament, she chases after Tenshinhan, who has gone off to find his master. Much to the disappointment of her many male fans, she has never returned.

See Glossary

Tenkaichi Tournament

See questions

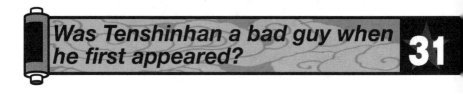

Was Tenshinhan a bad guy when he first appeared? **31**

Tenshinhan is human... although he has three eyes. Still, once you start pointing out little things like that, you have to talk about almost the entire cast of Dragon Ball! Most of them fly around the sky like it was something we do all the time.

Tenshinhan participates in the Tenkaichi Tournament as the pupil of Tsurusennin. He is an exponent of the killer technique Tsurusenryu, and indulges in a brutal fight, breaking Yamcha's leg. But this is done with little bad will, aimed largely at getting his revenge on Kamesennin.

He then faces off against Goku. At first it looks at though things are going Goku's way. But Tsurusennin's not happy with this, and uses Chaozu's psychic powers to help Tenshinhan.

When Tenshinhan finds out what's happening, he makes Tsurusennin stop, which in turn makes Tsurusennin mad. "Tenshinhan, you have defied me - me, your master!" he exclaims.

But Tenshinhan now realizes that he's a

See Glossary

Tenkaichi Tournament

103

true martial arts expert, and replies, "I just want to give my everything in this bout. I don't need any help. I can win with my own power."

When Tsurusennin orders him to kill Goku, he speaks his mind when he says, "I will not kill him. If I do then I cannot win this bout. And anyway, I don't want to be a killing machine."

When he witnesses his master Tsurusennin get blasted by Kamesennin's Kamehameha, he is relieved. "I have betrayed my master, but it feels like a great weight has been lifted from me. From here on, I don't give a damn about Tsurus, Kames or revenge. This is no longer a fight to the death. Let's concentrate on winning!" He then proceeds to fight fair and square.

After Goku suffers an unlucky defeat, Tenshinhan bravely admits, "I won because luck was on my side. On strength and merit, I would have lost."

Somehow, it makes it understandable why he fell for Lunch's craziness after she sneezed at him and became a crazed chick! Tenshinhan continues to train, and whenever the world is in a tight spot, he's always there, alongside Goku, ready to fight to save it from destruction.

See questions

7 8 12 21

22 30 45

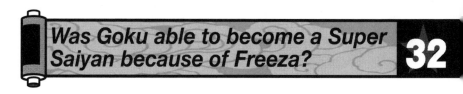

Was Goku able to become a Super Saiyan because of Freeza?

32

There are a lot of enemy characters in Dragon Ball Z, but one of the meanest, baddest and toughest is Freeza. Freeza speaks with a greasy politeness that shrouds a cold, calculating heart. He is the greatest and strongest of Goku's enemies. He uses his special army, the Ginyu Force, which he rules as a dictator, to search for the dragon balls. If his henchmen fail in their mission, he doesn't hesitate to threaten them with death.

When fighting, he can choose between three different power levels, converting up to face stronger opponents, who suffer mental as well as physical damage when beaten. He even manages to defeat Vegeta on one occasion.

Despite Freeza's obvious nastiness, Goku has Freeza to thank for his own increase in power. It was Freeza who was tough enough to withstand the Kaioken at a power of 20, and the massive Genkidama. Freeza's cruel killing of Kuririn, when he tore him apart, worked to fuel both Goku's anger and his power, and

See Glossary

Ginyu Force
Kaioken
Genkidama

helped him evolve into a Super Saiyan. The stronger the opponent, the more the Saiyan warrior aches to fight. Saiyans are also gifted with the ability to return in a powered-up form the more they are hurt. In this sense too, even though he probably wasn't aware of it, it was Freeza who made Goku develop into a Super Saiyan.

Freeza is beaten by Goku, but his body morphs into a cyborg. Returning to Earth to seek revenge, together with his father King Cold, he is killed by Trunks, who has returned from the future.

See Glossary

Super Saiyan
King Cold

See questions

Dragon Ball Collection Vol.1
Ginyu
$2.00

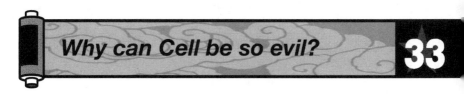

Why can Cell be so evil? 33

However way you look at it, Cell is one of the most powerful things around. No one can compete with his fighting power; not Piccolo, even though he has fused with Kamisama, not Vegeta, who is supposed to have outstripped the Super Saiyans, and not Trunks or Goku.

This is because Cell is the strongest, most evil android there is. He was created by Doctor Gero, the staff scientist for the Red Ribbon Army that Goku eventually destroys.

Synthesized with the cells of fighting exponents, Cell is believed to have been created from cells of Goku, Piccolo, Vegeta, Freeza and King Cold. He is driven by the need to become "the ultimate system," and he'll take as many lives as is necessary to achieve his aim, all without the slightest sign of remorse.

Piccolo is astounded by Cell's souped-up power: "Lord, how many lives did you snuff out to get your powers to this level?" But Cell merely replies, "Snuff out? They should be

See Glossary
Super Saiyans
Red Ribbon Army
Android
King Cold

proud to have become part of my power." He has not the slightest doubt about his right to maim and kill. And it's precisely that kind of skewed mentality, where things are immediately taken to extremes, which makes Cell evil.

Cell, the ultimate system, views the face-off with Goku as a mere game, hence the Cell Games, which he hosts. Cell draws on all that is evil, but is felled by the Kamehameha from Goku, who has finally awakened to his own amazing powers.

See Glossary
Cell Games

See questions

18 25 26 27
28 34 46

Is Mr. Satan nothing more than a fake?

34

Everyone knows Mr. Satan, because they believe he has come to save the world from its destruction.

Appearing in the Cell Games, he says, "I knew Cell for what he was the moment I set eyes on him. When it comes to fighting, he's nothing but an amateur. But fear not, Satan will blast away this stupid faker."

Mr. Satan, a mere human being, shows such confidence against his opponents that it seems to be a case of "lights on, nobody home."

But when he actually comes to face-off against Cell, super hero Satan, who carries on his shoulders the hopes of the world, enters the ring and is immediately blasted into a bloody pulp with one swing of Cell's right fist. Even then, he makes excuses, "I just slipped. No cause for concern. I'll take the fight to him...after a short rest."

Vegeta takes it all in, "Doesn't this guy realize that he's in a different league? World-

See Glossary

Cell Games

champion...and idiot."

Satan does play an unexpected part when Majin Buu appears. Although shaking with fear, he persuades Buu to stop his rampage. "You must stop all this killing and destruction. It just won't do," he says. Satan appears to know his limits on this occasion. But deep in his heart, he's screaming, "Yes! I am a super hero!! The world champion, Mr. Satan!"

Majin Buu, however, splits into two, with the "evil" Buu separating from the "good" Buu after Satan nearly gets killed. The fight that ensues between evil and good is a Dragon Ball Hall of Famer. Evil triumphs, and rightly so.

Satan then calls on Vegeta and Goku to concentrate all the power of mankind into the Genkidama...but the world doesn't listen. Just as it looks at though mankind will be annihilated, Satan loses all the cool he once had. "Listen up! Just cut the crap and start cooperating, Okay! You telling me you're not gonna listen to me, the one and only Mr. Satan...esquire?!"

So mankind concentrates its powers into the Genkidama, which, because of Satan's fighting words, now ripples with enough power to defeat even Buu, leaving Satan to emerge as hero.

But in typical Mr. Satan fashion, instead of

See Glossary

World Champion Idiot
Genkidama

accepting it all calmly, he puffs himself up and launches into a victory speech. "Majin Buu has been sent to his demise with your cooperation! You can rest easy! I have released you all from fear!" His daughter realizes what is happening and blushes pink with embarrassment. "God, Dad...you always get so carried away."

But let's not forget that it was Satan who originally tried to protect Majin Buu before he made the split into good and evil. "He's not such a bad guy," said Satan, "he's just going around doing all this 'cos real bad guys have told him to."

Mr. Satan may be shallow and a bit of an idiot, but when all is said and done, he's no doubt a hero and on the side of the good guys.

See questions

3 33 42

DBZ File 007

Boost Your Spending Power!

Tokyo merchandiser Cospa knew there must be an easier way to collect the seven dragon balls than roaming all over the land, fighting evil enemies and having to listen to Kami's bad jokes, and so decided to do something about it.

The answer? A Kamesenryu wallet with a chain that has all seven dragon balls attached!

Decorated on both sides with the Kame motif, the 10 cm by 13 cm wallet has a Velcro fastener, key-ring and sections for coins, bills and credit cards. But more importantly, it has a chain that carries all seven dragon balls.

Not only will storekeepers know you mean business when you pull out your cash, but now that you have all the dragon balls in your grasp, you'll never ever run out of money again. Not.

Wallet :$18.00
Chain :$32.00
http://www.cospa.com

What kind of kid is Goten? **35**

Son Goten, second son of Goku, is the spitting image of his father, from the way he talks to the way he does his hair. He has amazing power, equal, if not superior to that of his elder brother and Goku. He undergoes the same training as Gohan to participate in the Tenkaichi Tournament and becomes incredibly agile.

At the tender age of 7, he manages to become a Super Saiyan with seemingly no effort at all, a rank both his father and elder brother had to work hard at to achieve. He also masters Bukujutsu amazingly quickly.

He faces off against Trunks in the final of the youth tournament, only to lose. But his fighting powers astound all those present, as they are far and above anything normally seen in a child.

Goku disappears during the tournament, but Goten hears from Videl - Mr. Satan's daughter - that the reason is to prevent the evil wizard Babidi from bringing Majin Buu back to

See Glossary

Tenkaichi Tournament

Super Saiyan

life.

There then follows a comical scene in which there's no mistaking that Goten, although still a child, has the war-loving Saiyan blood running through his veins.

Goten, far from afraid, blurts out "That sounds like fun!" Trunks shouts, "You're gonna have to be quick if you don't want your old man to beat him up on his own!" Goten replies, "No way, no way, I have to see this! I have to get to see this Majin Buu guy for myself!"

In the final episode, Goten is 17 years old, and takes part in the Tenkaichi Tournament at the urging of Goku. But like any teenager, he tells his dad, "I'm only dong this 'cos you told me to. You're always so pushy! And I had a date all lined up for tomorrow."

Goten may be the spitting image of Goku, but he's also very much a modern kid.

See questions

7 17 18 26
28 42

Is Kaio greater than Kamisama? 36

Kaio is one of the Kaio Kings that rule the Galaxy. "Kaiosama stands over all the gods of the universe." In other words, he ranks above Kamisama, and is "all-seeing and all-knowing."

However, for someone with that kind of power, Kaio lives on a tiny planet with a pet monkey, Bubbles, and spends much of the time trying to convince himself, "I am Kaio, most powerful in the entire universe." He seems to have somehow lost the plot.

Kaio is fully aware that he's not ruler of the entire universe, as we witness when he tells the Elders of Namek, "I am Kaio, King of the Northern Universe. This is not my region."

When Goku is killed by Raditz, and before he's brought back to life with the dragon balls, he approaches Kaio to undergo further training so as to be able to take on new opponents. However, his initiation is strange to say the least.

"Oh ho, training is it then? Okay, I'll train

See Glossary

Bubbles

you, but you have to pass a test first. I consider myself to be one of the top funny-men around, so see if you can make me laugh!"

Goku is in a bind. The best he can come up with is a childish gag along the lines of, "What's the longest word in the world? Elastic! 'Cos it stretches for ever and ever." Surprisingly, it's enough to make Kaio burst out laughing. And he praises Goku, saying "I can see you're not just a pretty face. You could go places."

So Goku begins his training on the little planet with a gravity ten times that of Earth. By the time he returns to life, he has mastered the Kaioken. When he leaves, Kaio sends him off saying, "Well, there goes one guy with boundless power, yet his heart remains clear as crystal. To think that someone like that was running around down there in the lower regions. Still, he's not got much of a sense of humor. We'll have to work on that when he comes back."

Kaio can give the appearance of being dumb, but he sees through Goku in an instant.

See Glossary
Kaioken

See questions
2 4 6

When does Videl fall for Gohan? 37

After Cell kills Goku, the world passes through a period of peace. Gohan turns 16, and is attending Orange Star High School in Satan City. The city is named after Mr. Satan, who everyone believes saved the world.

One of the girls in Gohan's class introduces herself, "Hi, I'm Eraser. And this is Videl. You're not going to believe it, but her old man is none other than Mr. Satan."

Videl is extremely intelligent and has a deep-seated sense of right and wrong. Gohan does not reveal his true identity, but there are moments when Videl believes Gohan to be a warrior at the forefront of the fight for justice.

One day there is a robbery. Videl heads to the scene of the crime, where she proves her fighting prowess by facing down two of the robbers. "Just drop your weapons and come out quietly," she says, "That is, if you don't want to get hurt."

A fight erupts, and soon the Great Saiyaman - who's really Gohan in disguise -

See Glossary
Satan City
Great Saiyaman

117

appears on the scene and whops the robbers with a power that surprises Videl. But more surprising is how the Great Saiyaman know Videl's name!

Videl innocently asks, "Son Gohan, how did you manage to slip out of class?" And Gohan replies just as innocently, "Said I needed to pee, then managed to sneak off. Still, gotta get back..."

So Gohan blows his cover, and Videl follows up her searching questions with one that pinpoints Goku as the father of Gohan. Gohan is impressed. We may call it friendliness at first, but there's definitely an attraction growing between them.

Videl begins to learn Bukujutsu from Gohan and grows increasingly fond of him.

This we see when Gohan tells Videl," Your hair...I think you should cut it shorter," to which Videl blushes, saying, "Do you prefer short hair Gohan?"

Instead, Gohan reasons that it will be better for her to have short hair when she fights. At this, Videl loses her temper.

The very next day, however, she turns up with short hair, just as Gohan had suggested.

Her dream comes true when she finally marries Gohan, the scientist.

See questions

 26 33 34

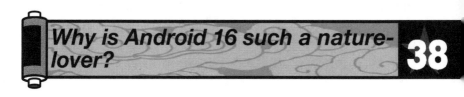

Why is Android 16 such a nature-lover?

38

Many peculiar android characters appear in Dragon Ball Z, but probably the most unfathomable is Android 16. He is the same perpetual energy type android as Numbers 17 and 18, but unlike them, who are "constructed almost entirely of organic matter based on human beings," his major feature is that he's a pure robot-type, "created from nothing."

According to Dr. Gero, his creator, "Number 16 is a defect," capable of destroying the world if ever put into use. His power certainly outstrips that of Numbers 17 and 18, and he's an equal match for Cell prior to him absorbing Androids 17 and 18.

Long after making his debut, he speaks for the first time when Android 17 asks, "You were also designed to kill Son Goku, right?" His answer is a laconic "Yes."

Although Android 16 starts out as an unfeeling machine of few words, he exhibits a quite unexpected side to his character when

See Glossary

Android

Vegeta fights Android 18. "See what you guys did," he complains, "You were making so much noise, you scared the birds away!"

He enters fighting mode to prevent Cell reaching Perfect Level, saying, "The time to fight has arrived, before I meet with Son Goku." He leaves Android 18, who he's known for only a short while, saying, "You're a good person. You never took the lives of humans or animals. It was good traveling with you." What a nice guy!

Android 16 is eventually torn limb from limb by Cell. But before he dies, he manages to make one last request to Gohan: "Please look after the animals and nature that I have loved so much."

It is said that we all want what we can't have. Android 16's love of nature probably derives from the fact that he's 100 percent robot, devoid of any natural elements.

It says a lot about the type of character Dr. Gero is, that he views this kindhearted android as a defect!

See questions

25 26 33 39 40 41

Why does Android 17 refrain from killing humans?

39

For Dr. Gero, Android 17 is "Forbidden Fruit." Kuririn rails at Android 17, "Just what the hell is it that you guys want? Are you looking to kill Goku, or just turn the world upside down?" To which the android calmly replies, "It is my intention to first destroy Goku. Then I will think about my next step. This is, after all, just a game, with Goku the strongest human."

Android 17 sets off to defeat Goku, but says to himself, "There is no reason to rush, let's take our time and relax along the way." He has energy to spare even after beating the likes of Trunks and Piccolo: "No cause for concern. They are both still alive. Be quick and feed them Senzu Beans, so that they can be resuscitated. Then if they can raise their powers, tell them I'd be happy to beat them again."

Android 17 may be an arrogant s.o.b. who manages to annoy almost everybody. But, in the end, he can be praised for never killing anyone. He is human-based, meaning the basic

See Glossary

Android

elements of his being are human-like.

We start to have our doubts about his penchant for evil when he defies Dr. Gero. However, even though Gero is the embodiment of wickedness, it doesn't necessarily follow that all who oppose him must be good. In the future that Trunks comes from, Android 17 comes across as an altogether nasty entity. But in this world, while he may be rather insensitive, he isn't necessarily bad.

Android 17 is capable of shifting from good to evil depending on subtle changes in the environment. In that sense, he can be described as the most human of the androids. He is eventually absorbed by Cell, but is destined to be brought back to life with the dragon balls. While this is not explained in so many words in the series, we know it to be true because Shenlong asks him to help the humans killed by Cell.

See questions

2 15 28 33
38 40 41

Why do Android 18 and Kuririn get married?
40

Android 18 is the twin sister of Android 17. Although obviously a female android, she resoundingly beats Vegeta in a one-on-one fight. She has incredible powers - even after a fight that leaves her clothes in tatters, she nonchalantly remarks, "I'm going to have to buy a new set of gladrags."

When Kuririn gets mad at Android 17, shouting, "Just what the hell is it that you guys want?! Are you looking to kill Goku, or just turn the world upside down?" and Android 17 replies boastfully, "This is just a game", Android 18 playfully kisses Kuririn on the cheek. It appears to be a spur-of-the-moment thing, but looking back on it, we see what a fated move it actually was.

There is an almost human quality to Android 18's spontaneous kiss. However, for Kuririn, who has little experience of the opposite sex, the kiss develops into something much more.

Android 18 is eventually absorbed by

See Glossary

Android

Cell. But in the fight against Goku that precedes this, Vegeta says maliciously, "If she's still alive, then kill her!" Kuririn attempts to protect her, saying "She's not so bad". To which Android 18, who knows Kuririn has the hots for her, cruelly replies, "Listen to the little shrimp! Wanna hold my hand or something, you little fart?"

Kuririn can't seem to get any respect from the girl he loves. Even when he gets Shenlong to remove the bombs planted inside the bodies of Androids17 and 18, all she can offer him is, "Hey, don't expect me to thank you for that bomb bit! Idiot!"

However, before she takes off, she does have kind words for Kuririn. "So, see you again," she tells him, probably the moment her feelings first tilt toward Kuririn. Eventually, of course, they marry and have a baby girl - Maron.

Although Android 18 is a cool, cynical young lady, she does have her down-to-earth moments, becoming the fussing money-concerned housewife. When she and Kuririn participate in the Tenkaichi Tournament in hope of winning the prize money is one such example.

See Glossary
Maron
Tenkaichi Tournament

See questions

2 7 9 24
38 39 41

How does Doctor Gero get killed by his own creation, Android 17?

41

D r. Gero is the scientist in charge of the Red Ribbon Army's android program, a role in which he plays the mad scientist to the hilt. He even appears as Android 20 - a revamped version of himself.

Buruma sees through Android 20 immediately, saying, "That's Dr. Gero! I've seen him in a book. But this is weird... I wonder if he's cloned himself..."

Dr. Gero returns to his lab and boots up Androids 17 and 18, only to have the latter ask, "You have also become an android, have you not?" Dr. Gero replies, "Yes, I've always wanted eternal life."

All starts going wrong when Android 17 escapes with the controller used to deactivate the androids in emergencies. When Vegeta and the others turn up at the lab, Android 17 ignores Dr. Gero's command to "Hurry up and deal with those guys", saying, "Do stick a cork in it, old man. We'll deal with them when we feel like it."

See Glossary
Red Ribbon Army
Android
Android 20
Dr. Gero's Laboratory

Androids 17 and 18 attempt to start up Android 16, but Dr. Gero tries to stop them, saying, "Don't you get it? After everything I've said? Whatever you do, don't hit the reboot switch!" Android 17 turns on Gero and tears him to pieces.

Dr. Gero's concerns about the wisdom of what he is doing are evident even when starting up Androids 17 and 18. "If possible, I want to avoid putting these two into action...I hope they're fixed," he remarks to himself.

At the root of these concerns is the fact that Dr. Gero has shifted too much of the workings of the androids to a perpetual energy furnace, making them increasingly powerful, and that robs him of control. What we eventually witness is the creator destroyed by his own creations.

See questions

20 25 38 39 40

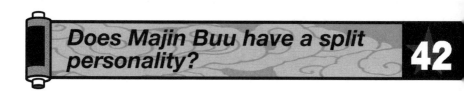

Does Majin Buu have a split personality?

42

ajin Buu is the strongest and most evil of all the bad guys. However, while he appears in the story as a fearless fighter, he's also something of a complete moron - a few beers short of a six-pack. Dabura, the king of the Demon World says, "God, this guy is just an idiot. Don't know how, but it looks as though I screwed up with this guy! I've waited for him for so long, but now he's here...I see that he's a brainless, powerless, gormless waste of time!"

Buu erupts with anger, blasting Dabura with a single blow. Gohan is amazed at what has just taken place and the power of Buu. But Buu is left with little alternative but to follow the orders of Babidi or else end up back in the ball from which Babidi released him.

Neither Kaio nor Gohan are any match for Buu, and soon both look set to meet their maker. After Dabura stabs Buu, he tells Babidi, "Mr. Babidi, Majin Buu will never be your faithful follower. Somewhere down the line, there'll

See Glossary

Dabura

come a time when you'll be unable to control him, and that will spell disaster for you."

But Babidi doesn't listen. Buu turns Dabura into a cookie and eats him. Babidi is the one who is driving Buu to commit one act of evil after another, and, in the end, it is Babidi who is destroyed by Buu.

Buu continues on his killing spree with little thought for what he's doing. Surprisingly, he treats those who aren't afraid of him with genuine kindness.

Mr. Satan appears as the savior of the world to defeat Buu...but ends up being befriended by him. So, when Satan, shaking at the knees, tells Buu that he must stop his killing, Buu's reply is trusting and childlike: "Okeedokee, no more killing then!"

However, when humans, looking to destroy Buu, attack both his dog and Mr. Satan, the evil Buu explodes. It is then that the two Buus emerge, as he splits down the middle, becoming evil Buu and good Buu.

Good Buu and evil Buu come to blows, but because evil Buu has acquired most of the power, good Buu is no match for his terrible twin. In the end, Goku amasses an extremely powerful Genkidama from the power of all humans and defeats evil Buu.

See questions

26 34

Why do Chi-Chi and Goku get married?

43

hi-Chi is the daughter of Gyumao. She meets Goku when they are both still kids, and Goku - who knows nothing - aims a kick at her groin. When he fails to get the same reaction he would have from a guy kicked in the same region, he reasons, "Thought so! No damned balls. You're a girl, aren't you!?"

This makes Chi-Chi angry, but she reckons that having being kicked there, the only thing she can do is marry Goku! So she says, "When I get older you gotta come and get me and take me as your wife." Goku - as thick as two short planks - says, "Get what? Don't know what it is you're offering, but if there's anything going for free, I'll be back to get it."

And that's how the two come to be married.

They meet again at the Tenkaichi Tournament. Chi-Chi is angry that Goku has forgotten her. Goku hasn't forgotten that he has to come back and get his wife...it's just that he

See Glossary

Tenkaichi Tournament

129

thinks a "wife" is something nice to eat. Still, Goku has never lied, and doesn't intend to start, so he says, "Okay, let's do this wife and marrying thing." And once again, he promises to marry Chi-Chi.

So the two get married. However, once she's given birth to Gohan, Chi-Chi turns into an education-mad mother. Part of the reason for this is that Goku, who's only concerned with fighting, never thinks twice about his wife. For her part, she becomes cold toward her husband and occasionally hysterical.

When it comes to the Cell Games, however, she warms to Goku, telling him, "Now, you look after yourself. And don't go doing anything stupid like dying." Unfortunately, that's exactly what Goku goes and does, leaving a young widow behind.

This causes her to be more emotionally attached to her child, becoming an overprotective, neurotic mother. She tells Videl, who is learning Bukujutsu from Gohan, not to overstep the lines of the teacher-pupil relationship "...and don't go offering your body as a way of payment!" However, she soon changes her tune when she discovers that Videl comes from a rich family. "So, when are you two young things getting married then?" she asks, embarrassingly.

See Glossary

Cell Games

See questions

7 17 26 33
34 37 44

Why are Chi-Chi and Goku so unhappily married?

44

oku was twelve years old when he first met Chi-Chi. They were both still children - innocent and unsullied. When Goku goes to look for Chi-Chi at the request of Gyumao, he invites her to ride the Kinto-cloud - the magical cloud given to Goku by Master Roshi.

"Let's see now. You can only ride it if you've got a pure heart," he tells Chi-Chi, who replies, "That's me! My heart's as clean as the flush in a toilet!" And it's true, as she proves by riding the Kinto-cloud.

Goku's heart is also pure. But, if anything, he's too naive. This is evident when he kicks Chi-Chi in the groin to see if she's a girl or a boy.

That angered Chi-Chi. "What do you think you're doing then?!" she shouts. Being a country girl, she decides the only thing to do after that is to marry Goku.

"You gotta come back and take me as your wife," she tells Goku. But he thinks a wife

See Glossary

Kinto-cloud

131

is something nice to eat, and says, "Don't know what it is you're offering me, but if there's anything going for free, I'll be back to get it."

They meet again at the Tenkaichi Tournament when Goku is 18. Goku, who has never told a lie, promises to marry Chi-Chi, but sadly their marriage turns out to be a loveless one. Goku has no real understanding of what marriage actually means, which is probably the fault of his Saiyan ancestry.

Throughout the entire Dragon Ball Z story, there are no scenes that link Goku with romance. Chi-Chi and her husband are doomed to a loveless relationship from the start. Goku can think only of fighting, and is often away from home training for more bouts. In a marriage likes this, it comes as no surprise to find Chi-Chi increasingly ignoring her husband and doting on her child.

Still, there are the odd tender moments between Chi-Chi and Goku. She shows genuine concern before the Cell Games when she tells her husband, "Now, you look after yourself. And don't go doing anything stupid like dying."

See Glossary

Tenkaichi Tournament
Cell Games

See questions

4 7 17 18
26 33 34 43
45

What about other characters that appear in Dragon Ball Z?

45

There are many other characters in Dragon Ball Z that have minor but important roles to play.

Oolong is a cute little pig that appears at the start of the tale. He's capable of transforming himself into any shape, and because of this the villagers are afraid of him. In fact, he's a bit of a weakling.

The cat-like creature that accompanies Yamcha is Puar, and she too can change into many different shapes and forms.

As well as father of Chi-Chi, Gyumao is known as the Wild Man of Frying Pan Mountain. He was once a student of Kamesenryu and a young follower of Goku's grandfather.

Chaozu, a Tsurusenryu follower who always hangs out with Tenshinhan, is gifted with supernatural powers. When a clash with Nappa puts Tenshinhan out of action, Chaozu steps up to the plate, only to be sent to his death by Nappa.

Captain Silver is a member of the Red

See Glossary

Frying Pan Mountain

133

Ribbon Army. He boasts, "I will snuff Goku out in five seconds," but is wiped out instead. General Blue is also a member of the Red Ribbon Army. He's a good looker, and catches the attention of Buruma, who makes eyes at him but doesn't get anywhere. She calls him gay, which makes him mad.

Tao Pai-Pai, Tsurusennin's younger brother, calls himself the world's number one killer. Hired by the Red Ribbon Army to fight Goku, he wins the first time around, but eventually loses. He attempts to take revenge after transforming part of his body into a machine, but is defeated by Tenshinhan.

Uranai Baba is the elder sister of Master Roshi, and can flit between this world and the next at will. She has the power to bring the dead back to life for one day only. It is at Uranai Baba's house that Goku weeps when he meets with the resurrected Son Gohan.

The Frankenstein look-alike, Android 8, was originally created by Dr. Gero as a guard for the Red Ribbon Army. But he hates fighting and befriends Goku instead. From then on, he becomes known as Hatchan.

See Glossary
Red Ribbon Army
Android

See questions

7 21 22 23
27 31 44

Why does Vegeta renounce fighting? **46**

Vegeta is an elite member of the warrior Saiyan tribe. He is a prince with strength, pride and a war-loving nature second to none. So why is it that after the fierce battle with Cell, he says, "I will fight no more?"

There are a number of reasons, the most important of which is that his archrival Goku has been killed by Cell. Having lost this worthy rival, there is nothing more to inspire him. We must not forget that Vegeta had set himself the task of being the one to defeat Kakarot (Goku's Saiyan name).

Another possible reason is that Vegeta may have felt his fighting abilities had reached their limit. At great personal risk, Goku transports Cell to Kaiosama's planet, only to die himself when Cell self-destructs. So, while losing Goku, at least Kaiosama has seen the destruction of Cell. Or so he believes. However, Cell is still alive, and goes on to kill Trunks, Vegeta's son.

Unsurprisingly, Vegeta challenges Cell to a fight, but he is dropped with a single kick. "Get screwed Vegeta!" says Cell, unceremoniously. And if that's not belittling enough for the Saiyan prince, Gohan is forced to come to Vegeta's rescue when it looks like he's going to get wiped out. Gohan is injured in the process.

Vegeta apologizes to Gohan, "To think that I would end up as a burden. I am sorry Gohan." This sense of despair surprises Gohan, "I never thought I would see the day when Vegeta would apologize."

When Cell kills Trunks before his very eyes, Vegeta goes berserk, causing him to act out of character and injure Gohan. This is a mistake, as Kuririn knows. "You total friggin' idiot Vegeta!" Kuririn shouts, "Trunks could have been brought back to life with the dragon balls!"

Vegeta is no longer the cool, cruel warrior that he was in the past. It was he himself who said that emotions should never intrude in his work. But his anger gets the better of him when he sees Trunks killed. It's a much greater shock than he initially realizes.

In the end, Cell is destroyed by a Kamehameha from Gohan, who has the support of Goku in Heaven. Vegeta is angry. "Damn those two!" he shouts, clenching his fist. "How could you go and die like that, Kakarot!" It is then that he renounces fighting.

Vegeta does participate in the Tenkaichi Tournament, the same one to which Goku returns from Heaven to fight in. They meet in the first round, and Vegeta is thrilled. "Yes, I've drawn Kakarot!" he tells himself, "This is what I have been waiting for! The day when I will have my victory over Kakarot!!"

But there is none of the evil or outright hatred that would have once made Vegeta scream, "I'm going to tear you limb from limb!" Vegeta enters the ring against Goku with a newfound sense of sportsmanship and respect.

See Glossary
Tenkaichi Tournament

See questions

2 7 18 28
24 33

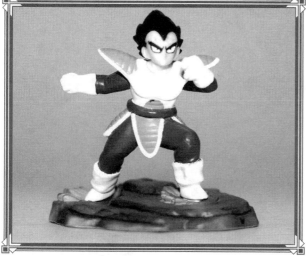

Dragon Ball Collection Vol.1
Vegeta
$2.00

Power Pouch

Once an essential part of modern day living, pouches are rapidly disappearing from the urban landscape. The pouchless are now in the majority, something that would have been unimaginable a decade ago, when everyone and his dog was pouched to the teeth.

But all is not lost. Tokyo's Cospa has a mission: To put the power back in the pouch. And what better way to it than with Dragon Ball Z!

Handy, hip and hairless, DBZ zip-lock pouches come in three cool designs: black-and-white Capsule Corporation, Goku-orange Kamesenryu, and Gohan's Number 4 dragon ball, also in orange. They're big enough to carry everything from a yo-yo to a pair of socks to a small animal. And each has an idiot-proof clip attached, which means you can hook it onto your bag, snag it through a belt loop, or even dangle it from your nose-ring.

Are You Pouched For?
Dragon Ball Z Pouch
$20.00
http://www.cospa.com

Who are the Nameks? 47

P iccolo has made such an impression on greedy Yajirobe that when Kuririn, Gohan and Buruma set off to Planet Namek to look for the dragon balls, Yajirobe fears the worst. "After they get there, what happens if they run into another 100 just like him?"

Kaiosama allays his fears. "No cause for alarm," he tells them. "Nameks are normally a very relaxed and easygoing race. Piccolo must have been influenced by some evil Earthlings he met before he became Kami."

Piccolo first realizes that he is not an Earthling when the Saiyan Nappa turns up. Piccolo and Kamisama overhear Nappa say, "My God, he's a damn Namek!!" Piccolo replies, "Well, well. Thanks for that. I now know who my ancestors were..." Kamisama chimes in, "Wow! I didn't know I came from outer space! That figures! Now I know why I've always felt different to everyone else!"

"So it's you lot who made the dragon balls, then?!" says Vegeta. Nappa blames Piccolo say-

See Glossary
Planet Namek

ing, "Those damned dragon balls are the main reason for me being here in the first place. Just hand 'em over right now, and no one gets hurt!" Piccolo plays dumb. "Ain't that a shame! Well, I'm sorry, but it wasn't me that made the dragon balls...I'm a fighter." Kami confesses that it was he who made the dragon balls "all that time ago...And even though it was the first time I'd ever done anything like that, there was a sense of deja vu about the whole thing. There must have been someone else on Namek who'd made something like dragon balls a long time before me. Somehow I managed to pick up on this as a distant memory."

Kami and Piccolo Daimao - the father of Piccolo - were once the same person. Guru, Grand Elder of the Nameks, channels into Kuririn's memory to discover that "he split after being infected with evil long, long ago! How stupid, to split the vast power he was born with... He might never have been killed if he'd had the power to reunite..."

Guru wasn't aware that there were Nameks on Earth, but learns from Kuririn, "Long ago...they came aboard space ships when their planet was destroyed." To which Guru replies, "Katattsu's son? Well, what a surprise, to think that kid made it here safely. Now I undertsand. He was a Healer and so capable of

See Glossary
Grand Elder

making dragon balls." The Healers (or Ryuzoku) are a Namek minority gifted with healing powers acquired from Shenlong. They make the dragon balls.

Another Namek group are warriors. These are highly skilled fighters whose role is to protect the Elders from invaders. Of the population of 100 survivors on Planet Namek, only one warrior is left. His name is Nail.

Although tough, Nail is easily beaten by Freeza. Piccolo comes across him as he lies wounded. Piccolo is amazed, "A Namek...Just like me!" Nail whispers, "God damn! Don't know what kind of training he had...But his powers are amazing."

Nail begs Piccolo to merge with him, telling him it will boost Piccolo's fighting powers immeasurably. But Piccolo isn't too sure. "Thanks for the offer, but not me! I work on my own. No way I wanna go all the way and combine my personality with yours."

Nail knows he is near death and pleads with Piccolo, "I have no time...I am going fast! Place your hand on my dying body...Don't worry. Your personality is your own. I am just setting the fusion in motion.

Piccolo has his doubts but chooses to join with Nail. And when he does, he can't believe it. "What incredible power!! So this is what it means to merge!!" He then flies off to where Gohan and his friends are facing down Freeza.

Gohan can no longer stand by and watch Freeza and his henchman Dodoria wipe out the Nameks. He goes to the help of the young Namek, Dende, who has supernatural powers of healing that save him, even though he suffers a near-mortal blow.

Dende takes Gohan and Kuririn to see Guru, who says, "I wish to thank you for saving my child Dende." As Guru is the possessor of various supernatural powers, we can assume that Dende has similar powers too.

Later in the story, Goku approaches the Nameks and asks them to send someone to be the new Kami. Dende is chosen for the job. One of the Nameks says, "Dende has always wanted to go to Earth ever since that time Gohan and Kuririn fought Freeza. He keeps saying he wants to meet up with them again. He may look like he's just a kid, but he's a fully grown Healer. He will make you a fine Kami!" "That's good! Don't let us down Dende," Goku tells him.

Dende doesn't possess strong fighting abilities. But he does have another crucial ability: the power to heal. He can also create dragon balls. Still, him being chosen to become Kami raises the question: What are Gods in Dragon

See Glossary

Fusion

Android

Ball?

They have no religious background. Out in the universe, there are many creatures superior to God. At the same time, there are characters such as Kaio, who lives for bad jokes and girly mags.

Kami has always been a Namek, and so Dende taking on the role is not out of character. While the Nameks appear to have a deep connection with Earth, they remain a mysterious people, which is probably what makes them so interesting.

Dragon Ball Collection Vol.1
Piccolo
$2.00

DBZ File 009

Dragon Ball - A $30-Billion Industry

Dragon Ball is now an international industry. It is estimated that since Goku made his debut in the pages of Shonen Jump in 1984, the series and its innumerable tie-ins have generated some 30 billion dollars. Japan, of course, is a major market - graphic novel sales have exceeded the 120-million copies mark, one for each Japanese person. But overseas, Dragon Ball has also met with success unprecedented in the world of anime and manga.

The Dragon Ball anime series is shown on TV not only in Japan and the USA, but also in another 40 countries, from Europe to S.E. Asia. This has driven sales in other Dragon Ball merchandise, nowhere more prominent than in the computer games market.

According to the Feb 17, 2003 Bandai sales report, the Dragon Ball Z game software compatible with PlayStation 2 had sold almost 2 million units in 20 countries worldwide. These included Japan, where it was released some four days before the Bandai report, the US, where it went on sale on Dec. 4, 2002, and Australia and New Zealand, where it came out on Nov. 28, 2002. Although nothing like these figures had been seen before, sales of the 26 Dragon Ball game software that preceded DBZ totaled some 11.5 million units.

In Europe, where manga has had to struggle against long-established comics such as Asterix and Tintin, DBZ was an immediate hit. Carlsen Verlag, the publisher of the German-language Dragon Ball graphic novel, reports selling two million copies of the manga since it was first released in Germany in 1997, far out-stripping sales of any other Japanese comic.

Who is the meanest DBZ dude? **48**

The Dragon Ball story can be roughly divided into two parts. The first part is about the search for the dragon balls. The second part describes the invasion of Earth by all sorts of enemies and how the heroes of the story respond to this in their quest for peace.

The common thread that runs through DBZ is that the good guys, such as Goku and Gohan, manage to defeat each new powerful opponent as he appears by undergoing disciplined training to increase their fighting powers.

Chronologically, the powers of Goku and Gohan are on a constantly rising trajectory, facing tougher tests each and every day as newer and more powerful enemies show up.

From this standpoint, and taking into account the fierceness of his fighting and his eventual defeat, we would have to say that Majin Buu is the toughest guy around.

Let's take a look at the tough top three

and who they are.

In third place, there's Freeza, who even managed to take control of the war-loving Saiyans. He intimidates his opponents with his feigned politeness. Freeza blows onto Namek looking to use the dragon balls to acquire eternal life.

He tells Nail, the warrior Namek who stands in his way, "Right! If you choose to stubbornly oppose me then I'll be forced to show you my ultimate terror, the most devastating thing in the universe! I'll tell you what I'll do...I'll fight you using only my left hand. That'll make things easier for you."

It's true that Freeza is incredibly strong and has confidence to spare, especially after testing his opponents strength with the Scouter, but everybody just loves to hate the guy! After tearing off Nail's right arm, he says in his usual malicious manner, "Now how did that happen? Sorry about that."

He's also capable of three transformations, powering up on each occasion. This includes his second transformation into a giant with incredible powers, which he uses against Vegeta.

At the third transformation level, Freeza is able to move at near supersonic speed. He attacks Piccolo, who has merged with Nail,

See Glossary

Scouter

using only his fingertips, and pummels him in a flash. In this final transformation, he shrinks in size, but his power is enough to make even Kaiosama flinch.

Freeza's struggle is against Goku, who has become a Super Saiyan. But Goku beats the hell out of him. With his pride in tatters, he turns to wiping out the entire planet. "What shame! Me, Freeza, taken to task by a mere Saiyan...and Goku of all people!"

Freeza returns to Earth once more, seeking revenge together with his father, but is easily killed by Trunks, who has arrived from the future.

Cell, with his awesome strength, is an easy second on the meanies list. Neither Piccolo, who has fused with Kamisama, Vegeta, who is believed to be even tougher than Super Saiyans, Trunks nor Goku are able to put up a good fight against Cell. This is because he's an android, created by Doctor Gero's computer.

According to Cell, long ago, Doctor Gero collected the cells of the greatest fighters and began research into synthesizing them. Although he gave up half-way through, his computer continued to process the information.

Cell was created with the cells of Goku, Piccolo, Vegeta, Freeza and King Cold, powering up even more by absorbing his opponents.

See Glossary

Android

King Cold

147

Also, in his aim for perfection, he absorbs the "Organic extract of several hundreds of thousands of human beings, using it as energy."

The Perfect Cell is unstoppable. He asks Trunks where Goku is. "Goku is training to beat you," Trunks replies. "He'll be here tomorrow to join the fight! He won't let you down. That much I know."

Cell announces the Cell Games ten days later. He comes up against Goku and suffers a mortal blow, but chooses to self-destruct instead. "It's all over for you too," he screams. "I self-destruct in one minute flat. I'll die, but I'll take you all with me...the entire Earth!"

Just before he self-destructs, however, Goku whisks him away to Kaio's planet, where both Goku and Kaiosama die along with Cell.

But here's the twist. Cell doesn't die. As he explains, "There's a small lump in my head that acts as my nucleus. As long as that isn't destroyed, my body can be recreated again and again. Luckily, when I self-destructed, that lump survived."

Vegeta attacks Cell after witnessing him kill his son Trunks. But Vegeta is no match for Cell. Just when it looks like Earth has had it, Goku contacts Gohan using Kaiosama's power. "You must give it everything you've got with your best Kamehameha," Goku tells Gohan. "If

See Glossary
Cell Games

you do, then you'll win. I promise!" Gohan puts everything he has into the fight, and with the added courage that Goku has channeled into him, he manages to destroy Cell.

Without doubt, the greatest enemy is Majin Buu, a creation of the evil wizard Bibidi. Majin Buu is like an animal, with no reason or emotions, and whose only purpose is to destroy and kill. In just a few years, he has wiped out hundreds of planets. He even kills three of the four Kaiosama that have the power to obliterate Freeza with a single blow.

Bibidi brings Buu to Earth trapped inside a ball, but he's killed by the surviving Kaiosama before he can break the ball's seal. Bibidi's son, Babidi, now appears, taking control of Vegeta, who wants to settle everything by beating Goku. The energy that is created when the two fight has the unexpected effect of bringing Buu back to life.

Vegeta feels responsible for resurrecting Buu, and goes after him. But although Vegeta's powers were awesome when he fought Cell, he's no match for Buu. It looks like the earth is doomed. But Vegeta has one last card to play. "Fire up the Genkidama!" he screams. "Let the Earthlings take responsibility for themselves once in a while!" With the compressed power of everyone on Earth, Goku releases the Genkidama, finally destroying Majin Buu.

See Glossary

Genkidama

See questions

2 3 4 5
18 33 34 39
40 42

It Figures!

For many Japanese, the words *gashapon* and *shokugan* bring back childhood memories of plastic lumps attached to candy bars to entice them to spend their precious pocket money.

Much has changed in the 20 years since *omake* first became widespread. No longer can manufacturers expect to palm barely-recognizable toys off on children in the hope of winning their consumer trust. Japanese kids have become both affluent and savvy, and now expect a freebie that greatly out-values the once-coveted bar of chocolate.

Dragon Ball Mini Figure Selection 2
Set of 16 characters. Each comes with its own labeled stand and two yogurt-flavor candies that carry the kame and 4-star dragon ball motifs. $1.50 each

This shift in buyer-seller relations has led to two significant changes: One, the products available today are increasingly detailed and well made, and two, many of them are sold as stand-alone products, having dispensed with the dubious sweet in the brightly colored wrapper.

It comes as no surprise to learn that anime figures lead the omake market, and the Dragon Ball gang is the most ubiquitous. From Coco Cola DBZ and the Dragon Ball Collection to Dragon Ball Capsule Battle of the Universe Freeza Series and Dragon Ball Fantastic Arts, the selection and brands are as numerable as the characters in the long-running series.

Of them all, the Dragon Ball Collection is of particularly high quality. 14 characters complete the set, including Oolong, Piccolo and Shenlong, although there are an undisclosed number of "secret" characters that will keep you guessing long after your money's gone.

Although no more than 2.5 inches in height, the figures are surprisingly detailed and well made. And what makes them especially appealing is that each stands on a base that slots together jigsaw-fashion with another character to create a realistic fight scene.

In the pages of this book, you'll find many examples of DBZ figures on sale in Japan. Inexpensive and remarkably true to the original, they have yesterday's children wishing they could be kids just one time more.

Dragon Ball Z Puchirama Capsule
A set of 6 characters: Goku, Gohan, Piccolo, Vegeta, Kuririn and Trunks. Each comes in a transparent plastic capsule with a selection of backgrounds. $2.00 each

Which characters were added for the TV series?

49

Some characters never appeared in the original Dragon Ball comics. They made their DBZ debuts when the TV series was aired.

Robot - The archeological survey robot that Gohan meets when he falls into the desert. Robot puts his life on the line to save Gohan.

King Moai - Despotic ruler of Arlian, the planet Vegeta and Nappa visit before Earth. Moai is killed by Vegeta, and the planet is eventually destroyed.

Princess Snake - The princess who lives in the castle on the Snake Way that leads to Kaiosama's planet. Although beautiful, in reality she is a giant serpent named Hebidojin. She tries to eat Goku while he's on his way to see Kaiosama.

Fake Saiyans - The Saiyans that Kuririn meets when he leaves Kamisama's palace and travels back in time. They are too primitive to be real Saiyans and are still rather ignorant. However, they possess advanced fighting skills.

Fake Nameks - As the name suggests, they are fake Nameks from a fake Planet Namek.

Garlic Jr. - The son of Garlic, who lost in the fight for the Kami's throne against Kamisama. He is the leader of the Four Dark Lords (Mazoku Shitenno, or the Spice Boys), and attempts to regain the position of Kami that his father so badly wanted. Instead, he gets sealed up in the dead zone, a dark anti-space of his own making.

See Glossary

Planet Namek

Four Dark Lords(The Spice Boys)- Spice, Zord, Tard and Vinegar. Spice is the most handsome of the four. Zord and Tard team up for a double-attack. Tard is best at moving and attacking from deep in the ground. Vinegar is the biggest dude of the four.

Haiya Dragon - Playmate of Gohan, he lets him ride on his back when flying.

Marron - Kuririn's girl friend. She has an amazing body that makes men do anything she wishes. Kuririn asks her to marry him, but is turned down.

Mr. Shu (Shusaiaku) - The tutor Chi-Chi hires for Gohan. He is really strict, whipping Gohan if he can't answer the extremely difficult problems he sets him. Mr. Shu believes himself to be the best tutor around.

Lime - The little girl who lives at the shop in Chazuke Village. Her parents are killed by Cell.

Laochu - A martial arts expert who once appeared in the Tenkaichi Tournament. He lives with Lime, and runs the shop in Chazuke Village.

Mister Satan's pupils - Caloni, Piroshiki and Pizza. They arrive at the Cell Games in a helicopter, presenting themselves as the saviors of the world. The beautiful Pizza is Satan's manager.

Pikkon - A martial arts expert from the western galaxy and a rival of Goku's from the nether world. He is easily capable of dispatching Cell and Freeza when they rampage through Hell. He fights Goku in the nether world tournament.

Daikaio - He oversees the four Kaio. A lover of the martial arts, he hosts the nether world tournament. He is usually to be found on Planet Daikaio.

Western Kaio - Controls the Western Galaxy. He loves gambling, and tries to bet on Goku's chances at the tournament

See Glossary

Tenkaichi Tournament
Cell Games
Nether world tournament

with Northern Kaio.

Eastern Kaio - The lady-Kaio who controls the Eastern Galaxy. She is overweight and a sore loser.

Southern Kaio - Controls the Southern Galaxy.

Angela - A classmate of Gohan's. He has his first date with her.

The Toto Family - A family of pterodactyls that live in the mountains and are friends with Gohan and Goten.

Muska - A circus promoter and crook. He steals the Toto child and turns him into a circus curiosity for all to ogle at.

Popeye - The hero of the Southern Galaxy. With the Southern Kaio, he spies on Goku while training and is astounded at the power Goku achieves as a Super Saiyan.

Bibidi - Father of Babidi, he also gave birth to Majin Buu long ago.

Daikaioshin - He oversees the four Kaioshin. He faces off against Majin Buu but Buu sucks him in and absorbs him.

Western Kaioshin - A very cute lady-Kaioshin.

Southern Kaioshin - Fights bravely with Majin Buu, but also gets sucked in and absorbed.

Northern Kaioshin - Also takes on Majin Buu, only to be killed.

Bardock - Father of Goku. A Saiyan warrior who opposes Freeza to the end. Looks down on Goku as a worthless lout with absolutely no fighting abilities.

King Vegeta - Father of Vegeta and King of Planet Vegeta. He is known as the strongest Saiyan, but is killed by Freeza.

See Glossary

Babidi

Super Saiyan

Participants in the nether world tournament

Olive - From Planet Earth. Appears as the representative of the Northern Galaxy.

Capita - Representative of the Northern Galaxy. He has ten arms, which he uses to tickle his opponents with.

Dolby - Representative of the Southern Galaxy. He has wings and is a skilled sky-fighter.

Maraiko - Representative of the Western Galaxy. A monster with a huge body and power to go with it.

Takapi - Also represents the Western Galaxy. He is small but can run like the wind.

Migoren - Also represents the Northern Galaxy. Not picked for the tournament, he supports Goku instead.

Arkua - Also represents the Eastern Galaxy. A merman-like character, he turns everything around him into water.

Chapuchai - Also represents the Eastern Galaxy. Outwits his opponents by dividing into two.

Sate - Also represents the Northern Galaxy. He once protected his homeland from a meteor.

Foolog - Also represents the Southern Galaxy. He has a face like a friendly frog and is capable of puffing himself up many times his real size, squeezing his opponents out of the ring.

See questions

7 18 33 48

Back in
the Real World...

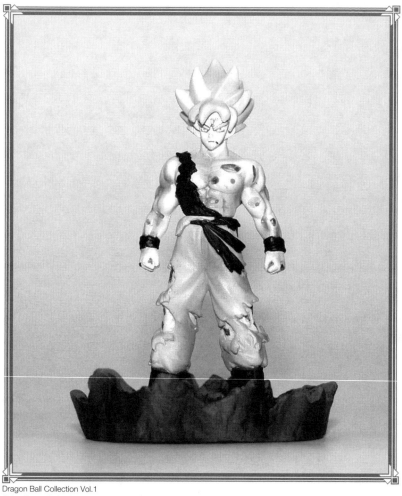

Dragon Ball Collection Vol.1
Goku (Super Saiyan)
$2.00

Who is the author of Dragon Ball, Akira Toriyama?

50

Akira Toriyama is one of Japan's major manga-ka, or comic artists. He shot to fame with "Dr. Slump," first published in 1980. Yet, Toriyama is also known for avoiding the limelight. He almost never appears on TV, nor in popular magazines.

In a rare interview, he explained why. "I'm the kind of person who wants to be able to just wander around, like at the supermarket, in my own time. There are plenty of things out there, and I just enjoy looking at them. A few years back, when I went to the supermarket, the girl on the cash register recognized me and asked for my autograph. I tried not to draw attention to myself, but ended up surrounded by old ladies! It took me ages to get away!"

Since then, he has consistently turned down offers for interviews and TV appearances that would reveal his identity.

Toriyama was born in Nagoya and has lived there all his life. He first worked as a designer for an advertising company, but found it almost impossible to get up in the morning. After three years and innumerable warnings about lateness, he quit.

Quickly running out of money, he turned to drawing comics, confident that he could sell his work. After entering a Shonen Jump manga competition, he received a call from the magazine's future editor. Although Toriyama didn't win, he was offered a chance to do a series. That was the beginning of his success story.

He last appeared in an interview in 1995, when the Dragon Ball series ended, but even then it was printed without a photo. A picture of him does appear on the cover of Volume 11 of the comic - a photo of him taken with his son Sasuke. But that was almost 15 years ago.

Toriyama is very down-to-earth for someone so famous. In one well-known incident, the truck delivering his work to his editor was involved in an accident, and some of his storyboards were subsequently lost. Toriyama, however, calmly blew it all off. "I made a copy. Will that do ?" he simply asked.

It's probably this ability not to be overly concerned with the small stuff that made it possible for him to complete such a long-running story as Dragon Ball Z.

See Glossary

Jump

How does Toriyama feel about Dragon Ball?

51

Because of Toriyama's reticence to be interviewed, we can only really get a glimpse of how he feels about DBZ from the few occasions when he has spoken in print or on TV.

In one interview, he talked about the early days of his career.

"Well, Mr. T - who was one of my early contacts at the magazine - knew I liked Jackie Chan, so he asked me if I wanted to do my own kung fu story. At the beginning, there were concerns that I might not be able to get it done. But I'm a sore loser, so I thought - Let's do it!

"Having said that, it was difficult coming up with fresh jokes week after week, which is why I turned it into a long-running story. That's when things really started getting interesting. The characters just about got up and walked around the page on their own. You might not believe it, but it really does happen.

"Anyway, I always thought I could call it

quits if things didn't go well. That's why I never really felt under any kind of pressure. I actually thought I'd take a bit of a rest after Dr. Slump...."

From this, we learn that Toriyama had no idea at the time that his series would continue for so long.

The overall Dragon Ball story is relatively simple, but Toriyama says he thought up the finer points and the endings as he went along. "That way, I could really enjoy wondering where I should go from here, and what I was going to draw," he said.

See questions

50

Toriyama undoubtedly ran into problems while creating DBZ, even though he's never mentioned it in public. But he clearly had a lot of fun as well, as is evinced by the continual word-play and the tongue in cheek connections to real-life situations found throughout the story.

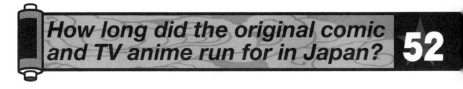

How long did the original comic and TV anime run for in Japan? 52

The comic "Dragon Ball" debuted in Shueisha's weekly Shonen Jump in the autumn of 1984 with the first installment "Buruma and Son Goku." In its first months, readers rated it as low as 15th in popularity, but it started to take off with the introduction of the Tenkaichi Tournaments. It ran until May 1995, almost a decade-long series.

Akira Toriyama, the artist, had always been prepared to end the series at any time in order to maintain its quality. The fact that it continued for so long is tribute to its loyal readership and its popularity.

The Dragon Ball anime series began on Fuji TV in February 1986, two years after it first appeared in Shonen Jump. Including "Dragon Ball Z" and "Dragon Ball GT," the complete series amounts to a total of 508 episodes, with three television specials and 17 movies.

Average viewing ratings for "Dragon Ball Z" over its nine years on TV were an impressive 20.5 percent. Episode 218, "Exposed!! The

See Glossary
Jump
Tenkaichi Tournament

Saiyaman Is Son Gohan" proved the single most popular, with an incredible 27.5 percent viewer rating. Even the 30th most popular episode garnered a 24 percent viewer rating. It is said that on a minute-by-minute basis there were ratings as high as 30 percent!

It was Toriyama himself who decided to add the "Z" to "Dragon Ball Z." Apart from having a zing to it, the "Z" was also included to affirm the status of the new program and to lay the groundwork for the move to the next stage in the Dragon Ball saga.

The animated TV series "Dragon Ball GT" ended after a run of 12 years on November 27, 1997, with "The Final Episode - Adieu Goku...Until We Meet Again."

See questions

7 8 9 50 51

Is it true that the anime series is different to the original manga? 53

Although there are original story lines that were added to both Dragon Ball and Dragon Ball Z TV series, they are based on the comic book story. The one big difference between the original manga and the anime series is Dragon Ball GT, which aired from February 1996. This is an original animated series and never appeared in print format.

In DBZ GT Episode 1, "The Appearance of the Mysterious Dragon Balls!! Goku Becomes a Child!?" Pilaf and his friends appear for the first time after a long absence. Goku reverts to a child in line with the wishes against the Dark Dragon Balls gathered by Pilaf. Goku, Trunks and Pan set off into space in search of the Dark Dragon Balls, which have been scattered far and wide. There they have many adventures and engage in numerous battles along the way. In the latter part of the story, Evil Shenlong appears, and Goku and his friends must face this formidable foe.

54 Did the same Japanese actor do the voices for Goku and Gohan?

Masako Nozawa didn't just do the voices for Goku and Gohan, but for Goten as well.

Nozawa is a veteran anime voice actor, and skilled at portraying boyish voices, such as those of Goku and his friends.

Her greatest talent, however, lies in near simultaneous voice acting of different characters. In DBZ, she excels in this, switching between the three characters with such ease that most recordings were done in a single take.

It must also be remembered that with all three roles, the timbre of the voice changes as the character grows from babies to boys to adults. Nozawa accurately conveys the same character as he goes through these transformations.

She is a professional, and much sought after in the industry for the rare skills required in differentiating between several on-screen voices at the same time, and being able to pull it off in a single take.

Glossary
and
Keyword Index

Glossary

139

Buruma fixes the Scouter left behind by Raditz when he comes to earth, and uses it to determine the fighting power of Master Roshi to be 139. Compared with normal human beings, who are measured at 5, this is incredible power. At the same time, Kuririn registers 206, Tenshinhan 250 and Yamcha 177. Kuririn is able to boost his power to 981 a year later when he fights Piccolo. But even then, he's controlling himself, and his reading is probably even higher.

4339 Years and 3 Months

The time it takes to reach Namek in the world's fastest spaceship, which is built by Buruma's father. Kamisama's ship can make it to Namek in just one month!

5.6 Seconds

The record that Master Roshi sets for the 100-meter sprint about the same time Goku and Kuririn begin training with him. Kuririn's time is 10.4 seconds and Goku's 8.5 seconds.

Android 20

The android Dr. Gero creates by revamping his very self. It appears he does it in an attempt to gain eternal life, but is soon unmasked by Buruma. She says, "You know, I think that is Dr. Gero himself. I've seen him in a bunch of photographs of scientists. Still, it's weird. I wonder if he hasn't redesigned himself?" 125-126

Android Controller

Androids 17 and 18 have an in-built emergency destruct device. Destroying them would prevent Cell from upgrading to Perfect Level. However, Kuririn falls in love with Android 18, and even though he has the controller, refuses to use it.

Android

Dr. Gero creates two different kinds of android. There are the perpetual types, such as Android 16, 17 and 18, which require no energy input, and those such as 19 and 20, that absorb energy. Goku has a hard time fighting 19 and 20, as they absorb all his energy.
25-26, 35-37, 43-45, 49-50, 87-88, 97-98, 107-108, 119-120, 121-122, 123-124, 125-126, 133-134, 139-143, 145-149

Babidi the Wizard

Son of Bibidi, the evil wizard who created Majin Buu though totally by accident. Majin Buu has incredible power, and in just a few years he reduces hundreds of planets to dust. But Buu gives even Bibidi a hard time, and he eventually seals Buu up in a ball. Bibidi hopes to take Buu to Earth and unleash him on humanity. However, Bibidi is killed by Kaiosama before he can break open the seal. Babidi takes over, bringing Majin Buu back to life. But Buu eventually turns on Babidi and destroys him.

113-114, 145-149, 151-154

Baldy!

What Chaozu shouts at Kuririn upon seeing his rounded head the first time they meet at the Tenkaichi Tournament. Kuririn retorts, "What about you? You've got no hair either!" But Chaozu takes great exception to this remark...pointing to the single hair on his head! Tenshinhan attempts to break it up saying "Cut out the stupid arguing...it's embarrassing."

Bankoku-Bisshorisho

One of the more dangerous of Master Roshi's killer techniques. In the guise of Jackie Chun, Master Roshi is the first person to use this technique at the tournament since Son Gohan, who raised Goku. It's so dangerous that when he uses it, he cautions his opponents, "Say give up as fast as you can. Otherwise you're gonna die!"

39-42

Bardock

Goku's real father. He is a brave Saiyan warrior who is believed to have fought to the bitter end when Freeza destroyed Planet Vegeta. Goku, having been put in a spaceship and sent to Earth, and then hitting his head in a fall, has no memory of his father.

Bashosen

A fan that Gyumao asks Goku to get from Master Roshi so he can put out the mountain fire. Goku and Chi-Chi jump on the Kinto-cloud and head for Kame House. The Bashosen can rustle up a mighty wind with just a single waft, thunder clouds with two wafts and a rainstorm with three. Having said that, the fan ended up being used as a pan mat and was thrown out after someone spilt soup on it!

Bora

The huge American Indian who protects the Karin sacred grounds. He is the father of Upa. A skilled fighter in his own right, he is killed by the world's number one assassin Tao Pai-Pai, only to be brought back to life by the dragon balls.

Bra

The younger sister of Trunks.

Bubbles

Kaiosama's pet monkey. Goku is ordered to try and catch him as part of his training, a difficult assignment given that the gravitational force on Kaio's planet is ten times that of Earth. Goku succeeds in catching Bubbles 40 days later.
27-30, 115-116

Buruma's Bust Size

At 16 her bust size is 85 cm. She says so herself!

Capsule Corporation

The company run by Buruma's father Dr. Briefs. It's so famous that even the policeman who gives Goku directions tells him, "This place is world-class." The corporation invented the Hoi Capsules that Buruma carries. They are capable of transforming into all sorts of things, including boats, food, time machines, cupboards, wardrobes chainsaws, bombs, houses and motorbikes.

Cell Games

The games that Cell hosts using the Tenkaichi Tournament as a model. It is his desire to gleefully watch, "Human faces twisted in fear and pain." The games are held at five locations 28 km from the Central Capital. Cell declares the tournament is open to all comers, but he swears to kill every single person on

the face of the earth once he has beaten them all in the Games.
107-108, 109-111, 129-130, 131-132, 145-149, 151-154

Cell Junior

In order to make Gohan mad, and therefore have him reveal his inner power, Cell pulls seven mini versions of himself out of his back during a fight with Gohan at the Cell Games. But what makes Gohan really angry is witnessing Cell pulverize the head of Android 16 after he begs, "Look after the animals and the nature I loved." Gohan totally destroys the Cell Juniors in no time at all.

Cell's Core

There is a small lump inside Cell's head that forms his core. From this, Cell can be reconstructed even if the rest of his body is destroyed. Using Instant Transmission, Goku transports Cell to Kaiosama's planet, where Cell self-destructs. However, the core remains intact.

Cell's Shell

Trunks' old time machine is found in the western countryside. Close by, there is the kind of empty shell a cicada leaves behind after it emerges from the chrysalis. This is none other than the empty shell of that most evil android, Cell. Cell had realized that the time machine was too small for him to operate, and so had regressed to an egg in order to ride it into the present. The shell is evidence that Cell is no longer dormant, but on the prowl in all his full-grown evil.

Curse that Seals Majin Buu
Majin Buu has no sense of loyalty whatsoever. Babidi forces him to submit by threatening to use a curse that will seal him in a ball. But Majin Buu grabs Babidi by the throat to stop him from saying the curse, and kills him in the process. Buu is now free to do whatever he likes.

Cymbal
The monster hatched from an egg spat from the mouth of Piccolo. His aim is to find the dragon balls. He's killed by Yajirobe, who slices him up and eats him.

Dabura
The evil king of the Demon World. Dabura possesses vast powers but becomes a slave to Babidi's magic. He is later killed by Majin Buu, who turns him into a cookie and eats him.
127-128

Dabura's Spit
Whatever Dabura's spit lands on turns to stone.

Daikaio's Life
Daikaio gets trapped in the Z-sword and so decides to give his life to Goku so that he may come back to life to save Gohan from the murderous Majin Buu. This means that while Goku will never again be able to die and come back to life, he will enjoy 1000 years of life.

Dirty Old Men
The first dirty old man that comes to mind is Kamesennin. Don't forget, his one condition for allowing Goku to train with him is to bring him a "Nice, ripe cutesy!" However, the Kaioshin of 15 generations ago also appears to fit the bill. He's really pleased when Goku tells him, "Don't worry, we'll let you have some real T&A," saying, "Really? Do you mean it?" Goku thinks of him as, "Pretty much the same type as Kamesennin." They are similar in that they're both old, with somewhat facetious attitudes, but also with incredible strength. The author's intent may be to add more humor to the story by making two extremely powerful beings dirty old men.

Dorian Airport, Papaya Island
The airport on the island where the Tenkaichi Tournament is hosted. As the name suggests, the tournament is held in a southern tropical location.

Dr. Gero's Laboratory

The lab is in a mountain cave near the Central Capital. It's where Androids 16, 17 and 18 are stored before Gero activates them to fight Vegeta and his gang. Gero is then ripped to pieces by Android 17.
125-126

Dragon Radar

Made by Buruma, it catches the faint radio waves emitted by the dragon balls, and flashes on and off to indicate their location.

Driving

How Kaio likes to pass his time on the small Planet Kaio.

Driving License

This is what Master Roshi produces by way of ID when Chi-Chi asks him for proof of who he is. At the very least, we know Kamesennin can drive.

Final Flash

The killer *ki* beam attack used by Vegeta to defeat Cell after he reaches Perfect Level. Vegeta succeeds in blasting away half of Cell's body, but because he contains elements of Piccolo, Cell is able to reconstruct.
25-26

Frying Pan Mountain

The mountain where Gyumao lives. His castle is on its peak, but the mountain catches fire while he is out picnicking with his children. He is unable to return home, and ends up defending the mountain from its base. Gyumao was once a pupil of Kamesennin (Master Roshi), and is the father of Chi-Chi, who Goku eventually marries.
133-134

Full Moon

Saiyans with tails turn into gigantic monkeys, increasing their fighting powers ten-fold, when they see a full moon. According to Vegeta, this transformation is not because of the moon itself, but because of the Brutz Waves contained in the light projected by the sun reflecting off the moon. At the time of the full moon, the Brutz Waves exceed the power of 17 million zenos. When that power is absorbed through the eyes, a reaction is set off in the tail. There are many planets in the universe, but none that gives off as many zenos as a full moon. However, there are a few Saiyans capable of artificially producing a moon that gives off in excess of 17 million zenos.
39-42, 47-48, 71-72, 75-78

Fusion

The process by which Piccolo and Kamisama merge to achieve an exponential increase in power. It is the young and powerful Piccolo who is

the base, and the fusion is set off as Piccolo touches Kamisama. When the process is complete, Piccolo says, "I am now neither God, nor Piccolo...I am a Namek who no longer knows who he is."
139-143

Galic Gun

Vegeta's killer technique. Similar to the Kamehameha, except that when released, the palms face outward.
25-26

Garlic Jr.

The son of Garlic, who lost in the fight for Kami's throne against Kamisama. Garlic Jr. is an original character created for the animated series. He gains eternal life from the dragon balls, but is sealed up in the dead-zone, a dark anti-space of his own making.

Genkidama

The killer technique Goku learns from Kaiosama. It works by concentrating energy extracted from grass, trees, humans, animals and the atmosphere, then releasing it in a thrusting force. Goku succeeds in recharging himself with the entire world's energy before creating a massive Genkidama with which he destroys Majin Buu.
25-26, 27-30, 47-48, 105-106, 109-111, 145-149

Ginyu Force

The vicious gang of ugly fighters created by Freeza. Made up of Ginyu, Guldo, Recoome, Burter and Jeice, the Force strikes a number of ridiculous fighting poses before and after each attack.
105-106

"Go for it Kakarot! You're the best!"

The sacred Planet Kaioshin is the location for the confrontation between Majin Buu, Goku and Vegeta. And this is when Vegeta, truly impressed with Goku, tells him, "You really are something." Vegeta is supposed to be a genius, but he finally realizes he will never be able to beat Goku. Vegeta has so far fought to kill for pride and pleasure, while Goku has fought not to win, but because he doesn't want to lose. While Vegeta once hated Goku's kind-heartedness, he now cheers him, shouting, "Go for it Kakarot!"
89-90

Goku's Appetite

This is something to behold! No one knows if all Saiyan's are the same, but Goku can eat and eat and eat... At the first tournament he participates in, Goku downs 50 helpings of Chinese food. He also scoffs the huge fish that Yajirobe had caught and cooked. This is one kid that likes his food!

Goku's Gender Check

Goku has been brought up solely by his granddad and knows nothing of girls. So, when he meets one, he pats her below the waist to check if she's a boy or a girl

Goku's Tail

As we find out later, it is his tail that proves Goku is not a human being but a Saiyan. It's also because of his tail that Goku changes into a huge monkey whenever he sees the full moon. The tail is also a weak-point, causing him to lose power and fold like a deck chair whenever anyone grabs it. Goku realizes this weakness and overcomes it by training - though we are not told how - and is able to carry on fighting even when Kuririn catches him by the tail at the 22nd. Tournament.
39-42, 71-72, 75-78

Golden Warrior

The crime-buster who suddenly appears in Satan City. In fact, it is really Gohan - who has just started high school - in disguise. He almost blows his cover when he forgets to remove his Orange Star High School badge

Goonies

Kamesennin's favorite movie. He has a video of it in his room.

Gotenks

The result when Goten and Trunks fuse. Although they intend to become a single super fighter, both parties are still kids, which means Gotenks ends up with a very innocent side to him.

Grand Elder

Considered the father of the Nameks, he lives on the Planet Namek's highest cliff to avoid attack. There he gives birth to eggs to ensure the survival of his race. He can read into the past merely by passing his hand over the subject's head. The Grand Elder also creates the dragon balls. He is sometimes referred to as "Guru."
139-143

Gravity Control Room

A room in Buruma's house where gravity can be controlled. Vegeta and Trunks use it for anti-gravity training.

Great Saiyaman

Concerned that his classmates might recognize him as the Golden Warrior, Gohan asks Buruma for help. Buruma uses her wizardry to design a retractable super-hero suit that Gohan can activate in an instant, allowing him to protect the city hidden behind a mask. Enter the Great Saiyaman!
117-118

absorbs, closer and closer to becoming the perfect being.
145-149

Pan

The child of Gohan and Videl, and the granddaughter of Mr. Satan. She participates in the Tenkaichi Tournament from the age of four, easily beating the huge Mou.

Participant Shen

He takes part in the 23rd Tenkaichi Tournament looking just like a regular guy. But he's really Kamisama in disguise. He fights Piccolo, but loses.

Peace and Justice

Piccolo seizes King's Castle and in a televised speech proclaims himself the new king. He tells his viewers that the words he hates most are "Peace and Justice." He does away with the police force and tells people to go out and just do what they want.

Piccolo Daimao's Coat of Arms

It's found after Kuririn is killed at the Tenkaichi Tournament. On a single piece of paper is written the character for "devil," or "ma" in Japanese. It is the same coat of arms prominently displayed on Piccolo's clothing.

Piccolo's Growth

Just before Piccolo Daimao dies, he lays an egg, out of which comes Majunior (Piccolo). Three years later, Piccolo takes part in the Tenkaichi Tournament. Even at this stage, Piccolo appears to be a fully-grown adult. So, is it true that Nameks grow faster? No, they don't, as Dende proves. However, although they are the same Namek race, Piccolo is a warrior, and that may be the secret of his rapid growth.

Planet Namek

Piccolo's home planet. Centuries ago, Namek was almost destroyed by a sudden climatic change. There are two types of Nameks - one have mystical powers that allow them to heal people and make dragon balls, the other are the warriors, represented by Piccolo, who are fewer in number, and whose mission is to protect the Healers from invaders. Gohan and Kuririn venture to Namek to search for the dragon balls and save Piccolo and his friends, who have been killed by Vegeta. But Vegeta and Freeza also seek the dragon balls...
23-24, 57-58, 139-143, 151-154

Planet Vegeta

Mother planet of the warrior Saiyans that exploded when a massive meteor hit it. Almost all the Saiyans on the planet were killed, apart from Goku - called Kakarot in Saiyan - who escaped.

73-74, 75-78, 93-94

Polunga

The dragon created by the Grand Elder of Namek. His name means "God of Dreams" in the Namekian tongue. He can grant up to 3 wishes and can call back to life someone who has died more than once, but, unlike Shenlong, he cannot resuscitate many people at one time with just one wish. He can be summoned every 130 days, the same number of days needed by the Namek Dragon Balls to reactivate themselves.

Potala

The earrings that Daikaiosama gives to Goku together with the gift of his life. By having your partner wear one earring of the pair, and you the other, it's possible to achieve a power that outdoes even that of fusion. The Potala earrings have been a Kaioshin treasure for many years. Goku intends to use them to fuse with Gohan when he returns to Earth. But Majin Buu absorbs Gohan, leaving Goku to fuse with his one-time rival Vegeta to emerge as the powerful warrior Vegetto.

Rabbit Army

The name of the group that terrorizes a small country town, walking around acting like they own the place. Their boss is Toninjinka, who is able to turn anyone into a carrot just by touching them. Goku is done in this way and ends up making rice cake on the moon.
21-22, 51-53

Red Ribbon Army

The most evil army in history, feared even by the police. Under Commander Red, they plan to conquer the world. They pay Tao Pai-Pai to assassinate Goku and seize the dragon balls. They also delegate all power to Dr. Gero in his project to develop the androids. Androids 16, 17, and 18, along with Cell later in the series, are all developed as part of this project. The reason why Commander Red wants to get the dragon balls is that he wants to add a few inches to his height to be popular with the chicks. Red is eventually killed by his advisor Black.
83-84, 107-108, 125-126, 133-134

Rogafufuken

Yamcha's technique. The first time we meet Yamcha, he's an outlaw, making his living by stealing from those who get lost on the plains. When he faces off against Goku he leads with this technique, which involves attacking with claw-like punches and kicks and finishing off with a double-fisted "claw-punch."

Royal Defense Force

Equipped with the latest in fighters and tanks, the force's mission is to

protect the country. But there is nothing they do can in the face of Vegeta, Freeza, the android Cell and Majin Buu.
21-22

Sacred Water

This is different to the bogus tap water that Karin claims is special. This is the real thing. It can be used to bring out the powers that lie deep within oneself. However, because of this, it is also a dangerous poison. Those who do not possess superman strengths, highly developed mental powers and strong *ki* energy will die as soon as they drink it. It is said that even Karin ends up throwing up when he first drinks it. Goku takes the sacred water little by little, building up his resistance as he sets his sights on defeating Piccolo
27-30

Saibaiman

When the Saiyan Nappa comes to Earth, this is the character that sows seeds that grow immediately into little monsters. He has a fighting power of 1200, but is beaten by Piccolo and Kuririn.

Satan City

The town where Mr. Satan lives. Everyone believes that he saved the earth...But we know it's not true.
117-118

Scouter

Brought to Earth by the invading Saiyans. An opponent's fighting capability can be measured through this monocle-like apparatus, which hooks over the ear. When Raditz arrives on Earth, the power level of the average male human is a mere 5. Freeza has a reading of 53 even before he powers up. Who can say what his reading is after he defeats Goku and Trunks? In the Japanese version, Scouter is called Scounter (S-Counter, or Strength Counter).
31, 61-62, 145-149

Shinkikoho

Tenshinhan's favored technique, the awesome power of which he blasts Cell with even as it drains him of *ki* energy.
25-26

Special Life Forms

A computer calculated that for Cell to reach Perfect Level, it isn't sufficient to simply absorb organic essence. He must also absorb special life forms. This he does, absorbing Androids 17 and 18.

Spirit of Vegeta

Enma Daio decides to keep the spirit of the dead Vegeta, just in case he needs it. To allow it to fight Majin Buu, he gives it flesh and orders it to go save the earth.

Spy Robot

A small bee-like robot developed by Dr. Gero to collect the cells of the leading fighters. The synthesized android produced from these cells is, of course, Cell. The robot also spies on its subjects.

Staple Namek Diet

Piccolo and Dende take only water. How they are able to generate such power from this is a mystery.

"Strong and hardy, but more than anything else, pure of heart"

Only those who Karin judges meet these conditions are allowed to visit Kamisama. Karin recognizes these conditions in Goku. And that is how Goku sets off for the palace to ask Kamisama to resurrect Shenlong, so that all those killed by Piccolo may be brought back to life.

Super Saiyan

Legend has it that once every 1000 years, an ultimate Saiyan warrior emerges who can surpass all limits to become so powerful that he can destroy the universe. Vegeta is the first to realize that the legend is true. Goku, Vegeta, Gohan and Trunks all have the capabilities to become Super Saiyans, but it is Goku who is the ultimate Saiyan.

105-106, 107-108, 113-114, 145-149, 151-154

Super Saiyan 3

The form into which Goku changes to face off against Majin Buu. He first transforms into a Saiyan, then into a Super Saiyan, and eventually to a Super Saiyan 3. The *ki* force he releases is enough to rattle the planet, and vibrations can be felt as far away as Kaioshinkai.

Super-Dodonpa

The killer technique unleashed by the world's-number-one-assassin-turned-Cyborg, Tao Pai-Pai, at Tenshinhan at the Tenkaichi Tournament. But Tenshinhan has been training hard and is able to deflect the blow with will power alone.

Taiyoken

Another Kuririn technique, it's a bright light that shines out from his forehead, blinding opponents.

Tenkaichi Tournament

A tournament held once every few years in the south to decide the number one martial arts fighter from among the many challengers. Goku first participates in the 21st tournament.

27-30, 35-37, 39-42, 43-45, 51-53, 61-62, 81-82, 83-84, 85-86, 97-98, 101-102, 103-104, 113-114, 123-124, 129-130, 131-132, 135-137, 151-154, 161-162

"Those few months we spent together? They weren't bad kiddo."

The words Piccolo utters just before he dies after saving Gohan from Nappa. In the few months Piccolo trains Gohan to resist an invasion by the Saiyans, he becomes very fond of the young warrior.
95-96

Three Eyes of Tenshinhan

Tenshinhan has three eyes. But this hardly makes him strange in a world where a dog is king, and monsters talk.

Umigame

Umigame meets up with Goku after getting lost and wandering about on land for an entire year while picking mushrooms. Goku puts him back in the sea. As a way of thanking Goku, Umigame introduces him to Kamesennin. It is then that Goku receives the Kinto-cloud.

Uub

The reincarnation of the evil Majin Buu.
35-37

Viral Heart Disease

According to Future Trunks, who has arrived from 20 years in the future, Goku dies of a viral heart disease. However, the future is such a miserable place that Trunk's mother,

Buruma, constructs a time machine to send her son back to the present. There he hands Goku a cure for the incurable virus that will eventually kill him.

World Champion Idiot

Mr. Satan names himself champion of the martial arts world. But when he takes part in the Cell Games, he's blasted off his feet by a single blow from Cell. Satan rises from the canvas to say, "No problem... Once I've caught my breath, I'll come out really fighting." Vegeta cannot believe what an idiot Satan is and so nicknames him, "World Champion Idiot."
109-111

Yardrats

Goku manages to escape Namek on a Ginyu space pod that is programmed to proceed directly to the Planet Yardrat. Yardrats, the inhabitants of the planet, are not very powerful, but they know many fighting techniques, and teach Goku the Instant Transmission.

Yoikominminken

The technique used by Master Roshi in the guise of Jackie Chun when he faces off against Goku at the Tenkaichi Tournament. The technique uses hand movements, the power of the eyes and lullabies to lull the opponent to sleep. It's not so much a fighting technique as a form

of hypnosis.
39-42

Z-Sword

The legendary sword kept on the sacred Kaioshinkai, the planet supposedly off-limits to all but the Kaioshins. The Z-Sword has been thrust into the peak of a hilly crag and no one has yet been able to pull it out. Whoever removes it from the rock face will be rewarded with incredible powers, exceeding even those of Majin Buu. Super Saiyan Gohan successfully extracts the sword, but the blade splinters and disintegrates when he attempts to slice what is reputed to be the hardest material in space - Kachinko. Suddenly, an old man appears. It turns out that he was sealed in the sword some 15 generations ago by the Kaioshins.

Zeni

The Dragon Ball currency. Given that Goku ate 50 helpings at a Chinese restaurant and paid 470,000 zeni, that would put the exchange rate somewhere around 3 zeni=1 yen.
21-22, 35-37, 43-45

Cosplay Girls
Japan's Live Animation Heroines

All over Japan, hard-core fans of anime, games and manga are hitting the streets in their latest cosplay outfits - especially girls! And cosplay is now catching on fast overseas. Inside **Cosplay Girls** you'll find tough street-fighting chicks, emerald-haired princesses, spunky school girls and faux-fur kittens. This full-color glossy book is also packed with info on the characters they portray, how to pose, and methods of making and wearing costumes. As well as a fun guide to games, manga and anime big in Japan, **Cosplay Girls** also highlights the creative powers of Japanese otaku girls.

$19.95   ISBN 0-9723124-7-1

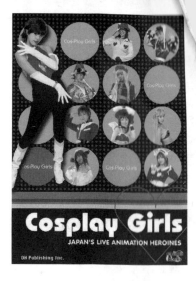

Secrets of the Ninja
Their Training, Tools and Techniques

Now you see them, now you don't. Peek inside the ninja's world and discover the skills, weapons, and ingenious tricks that made these men and women feared and revered for centuries. Learn ninja techniques for meditation, stealth and fighting dirty. Study their diet, ancient codes, workout and accupressure points. With **Secrets of the Ninja**, unravel the many mysteries of the enigmatic ninja and find out what it really meant to be one in old Japan.

$19.95   ISBN 0-9723124-6-3